The Elements of Teaching

The Elements of Teaching

Second Edition

James M. Banner, Jr.,
and Harold C. Cannon

Foreword by Andrew Delbanco

Yale

UNIVERSITY PRESS

New Haven and London

Published with assistance from the foundation established in memory of
Philip Hamilton McMillan of the Class of 1894, Yale College.

Yale University Press books may be purchased in quantity for
educational, business, or promotional use. For information,
please e-mail sales.press@yale.edu (U.S. office) or
sales@yaleup.co.uk (U.K. office).

Designed by Sonia L. Shannon.
Set in Fournier type by Newgen North America.
Printed in the United States of America.

Library of Congress Control Number: 2016941944
ISBN 978-0-300-21855-8 (paper : alk. paper)

A catalogue record for this book is available from the British Library.

This paper meets the requirements of ANSI/NISO Z39.48-1992
(Permanence of Paper).

10 9 8 7 6 5 4 3 2

✎ Contents

✥ *Foreword*

ONE COULD spend a lifetime reading books about education and never come close to getting through them all. Ever since Plato took up the subject nearly two and a half millennia ago, there has been a flow of commentary on what and how to teach. Today it's a flood. Libraries and bookstores replenish themselves continually with books explaining what's wrong with our schools and colleges and how to fix them. Some such books are popular, others technical, but most are quickly forgotten. James M. Banner, Jr., and Harold C. Cannon's *The Elements of Teaching* is a notable exception—a wise and wonderfully concise reflection on a subject about which one might think everything worth saying has already been said.

First published in 1997 and reissued now with a few revisions, mostly light, it will strike some readers as a book retrieved from the past. "We do not," the authors then wrote, "ask teachers to convey information," which is something we get "from newspapers, the stock market ticker tape, or price tags on items in a store." Yes, this list is outdated. Over the past twenty years, as everyone knows, newspapers have struggled for survival, ticker tape has become a relic of the predigital age, and price tags have been replaced by bar codes. This book was conceived before Google and Wikipedia turned the world into one vast reference room accessible, as the phrase goes, 24/7.

But the deep technological changes we have lately witnessed only underscore the urgency of what Banner and Cannon have to say. At a time when more and more educational policy makers are seized by the vision (utopian to some, dystopian to others) of technology as the key to making schools and colleges more efficient, this book is a reminder that the one indispensable element for every student is an engaged and committed human—and humane—teacher. "Presence matters," as Gary Saul Morson (a distinguished literature professor at Northwestern University) and Morton Schapiro (an equally distinguished economist and president of that university) have recently written. Banner and Cannon have mounted a passionate defense of this truth at a time when, strange to say, it is being disputed or forgotten.

They mean a particular kind of presence—that of a teacher for whom teaching is a "calling" and "an act of faith." True teachers, they write, are "missionaries for their subjects." The kind of teachers they have in mind are people in love with their subject whatever it may be—people bursting with delight in sharing it with younger people in the hope that their own pleasure will be catching. And if Banner and Cannon are partial to the language of religion, they dare to draw as well on the language of eros. "Teachers, in showing their students how to learn, must seek to be caught *flagrante delicto* with their subject. . . . The pleasure of teaching," they write, "is reciprocal: as teachers feel pleasure by giving it, students gain pleasure and return it by pleasing their teachers." Some readers will be wary of this formulation at a time when, for good reasons, any hint of sensuality carries a strong negative charge if applied to the relation between students and teachers. Lest there be any confusion, Banner and Cannon make clear that "teachers should never be students' close friends or companions" much less "their intimates."

Yet students are most likely to discover the pleasure of learning by witnessing teachers in the throes of pleasure ("the teachers whom we remember most vividly are those who knew their subjects best and transmitted them with the greatest intensity and love") as they move through the steps of a mathematical proof, or the verses of a poem, or the idioms of a foreign language. Such teachers have mastered their discipline, yet they are patient with novice learners. They are driven by the belief that *all* students have the capacity to become "more knowledgeable, more open to life, more understanding of the world than when they first entered the teachers' classrooms." The ideal of universal awakening implicit in this credo may seem impossibly naïve in a world where more and more stress is placed on sorting students into ranks of proficiency through one kind of test or another, but it is a basic tenet of democracy that all people have the potential and right to develop their talents in an environment of support and dignity. This book is a moving affirmation of that conviction.

In order to advance their work, teachers must possess great reserves of empathy. They "must recall their own earlier vulnerabilities to influence, their own difficulties in learning, and their own anxieties about acceptance and popularity." They must "put themselves in their students' places, . . . and then . . . help those students imagine themselves in other times, locations, and circumstances not immediately present to their senses." These sentiments may seem to apply mainly to teachers working with schoolchildren or adolescents, or, perhaps, with tentative college students afraid of failure under the pressure of competitive peers—and of course the challenges of teaching at different levels can be very different. For high-achieving students in elite universities, a main obstacle to learning may be the paralyzing pressure to achieve still more; for children in a prekindergarten program, it may be adjusting to a place ruled by adult strangers. Yet Banner and Cannon speak to the commonalities. Historian and classicist, respectively, they have taught over many decades in contexts ranging from inner-city schools to highly selective universities, and one of the striking aspects of their book is its pertinence to teachers of whatever subject at whatever kind of institution.

It is also striking that two scholars so much engaged with the past have written mainly in the present tense. With its combination of general pedagogical principles and portraits of particular teachers at work, their book confirms that all basic educational problems are both old and new. Teachers who last more than one season face an annual wave of new students who remind them that they, the teachers, have grown up in a world which, for students, already belongs to the unknown or barely known past. Since the pace of change now accelerates exponentially rather than incrementally, the gap between the formative experiences of teachers and students may be larger today than ever before—but there has always been a gap. And yet a gifted teacher can reduce if not close it.

Here, as quoted by Banner and Cannon, is the philosopher William James, a college professor whose presence in the classroom was famously magnetic, writing at the turn of the twentieth century about every teacher's obligation and opportunity:

> In teaching, you must simply work your pupil into such a state of interest in what you are going to teach him that every other subject of attention is banished from his mind; then reveal it to him so impressively that he will remember the occasion to his dying day; and finally fill him with devouring curiosity to know what the next steps in connection with the subject are.

Today we might translate these remarks into the observation that a good teacher is the best antidote for what we call "attention deficit disorder," a malady from which all of us suffer to one degree or another in our "multitasking" society, and to which the best response is the kind of intense and infectious concentration on something—almost anything—which a good teacher exemplifies.

Banner and Cannon are also well acquainted with, and uncommonly articulate about, the perennial paradoxes of the classroom. Teachers, they know, must walk the fine line between demand and encouragement, between approachable informality and impenetrable formality. They must realize that good teaching works through earned authority rather than exerted power, that it is characterized by professional confidence tempered by humility, and above all by not trying to force students to learn but by inspiring them to *want* to learn.

Some will say that such fluffy generalities won't do us much good at a time when we need tough responses to hard problems.

This is not a book for policy wonks. It says nothing about the hot issues of our day: the merits of charter schools versus traditional public schools; the pros and cons of standardized testing; how exactly to measure the quality of teaching and learning; whether to defend or dispose of tenure as a professional norm, to name just a few. For discussions of those issues readers will have to turn elsewhere, and there are plenty of places to turn. What they will find in this book is, instead, a tonic for both aspiring and veteran teachers who know that theirs is a profession less exalted and less well compensated than many others, yet potentially more rewarding.

"Most teachers forget," Banner and Cannon write in the opening sentence of the book, "that teaching is an art." Most books about education forget this too. There are, of course, exceptions. I think of Mike Rose's *Why School?* (2009), a bracing account of how even ill-prepared students can thrive under the guidance of dedicated teachers. Among books concerned specifically with colleges and universities, I think of Elizabeth Samet's *Soldier's Heart* (2007), about teaching literature at West Point, of Patrick Allitt's *I'm the Teacher, You're the Student* (2004), an account of teaching history to undergraduates at Emory University, of Mark Edmundson's *Why Teach?* (2013), a defense of the putatively "useless" liberal arts by a professor at the University of Virginia. And there are certainly others. But most books about education these days focus on the conditions of institutions—on their insupportable cost, their wastes and failures, or on their threatened worth at a time of rising public frustration and even rage.

All these issues are as tangled as they are important—and, indeed, the kind of teaching Banner and Cannon celebrate will only be carried on if we reorder our national priorities to make the investments necessary for ensuring the vitality of education at all levels. Still, at the end of the day, even if we somehow manage to fix the daunting structural problems, the single most important factor in every student's experience will continue to be the quality and commitment of his or her teacher. This book is a testament to that truth.

Andrew Delbanco
June 2016

❧ Preface to the Second Edition

THE IDEA of issuing a second, twentieth-anniversary, edition of *The Elements of Teaching* originated with Yale University Press, not with us. The Press's justification, gratifying to be sure, was that this little book had continued to find readers over two decades and, in addition, had been translated into Arabic, Chinese, Korean, Vietnamese, and French. We readily complied with the Press's request to undertake what was required for another edition because it gave us the chance to make a few desirable small changes in the original text and to add a new chapter.

Choosing principally to correct minor errors and alter a few infelicities, we have kept changes to the first edition to a minimum. The principal addition to the earlier version is the single chapter on tenacity and the replacement of one sketch, which we came to believe was too harsh a negative depiction of the original character in the chapter on ethics.

A few readers and reviewers have remarked, sometimes in praise, sometimes in condemnation, that the book is old-fashioned, and we admit without embarrassment that they are correct. In extenuation, we insist that the classic characteristics of good teaching do not change from one generation to the next. Had we written a book about methods of teaching, the contents of such a work would have been entirely up-to-date.

The elements of teaching which we describe are also always up-to-date—but up-to-date by being traditional.

One aspect of what we originally wrote is now clearer to us than it was twenty years ago: the inextricable interconnectedness of all of the elements of good teaching. That feature of teaching was implicit in what we wrote, and occasionally we pointed it out. Yet to make more explicit what we wrote earlier would require a more thorough revision of the whole, something not asked of us. We therefore make modest amends here by insisting on the reality that none of the elements of effective teaching stands alone.

We renew our thanks to those acknowledged in the first edition, some of them now deceased. To those named there we gratefully add Sarah Miller of Yale University Press, the editor who has guided us through this revision, and we renew our earlier tribute to our peerless copy editor, Dan Heaton, who, twenty years on, has once again applied his skilled eye, mind, and pen to the text.

❧ Preface to the First Edition

THIS BOOK is about teaching. And because it is about teaching, it is devoted to the personal qualities of good teachers.

Believing that teaching is an art, we have emphasized the artists who practice it. This does not mean that we are unmindful of the science of teaching; as with every other art, mastery of teaching is gained through close attention to methods and materials as well as to refinement of native gifts. Yet we have focused on the qualities, both natural and cultivated, of those who teach rather than on the techniques they use because far too much attention has been given to explaining the process of teaching and not nearly enough to describing the people responsible for that process. Those people cannot be separated from what they do. The human factor in teaching is infinitely variable and beyond the reach of scientific inquiry. It is that factor, rather than the professional one, that is the subject of this book.

We have written it for those who teach and for those who wish to consider what makes up the art of teaching and learn to recognize its achievement. Who, specifically, do we have in mind as our readers?

❧ Those who are considering teaching as a career or just beginning to teach, who need to know both the demands of their chosen work and the deep satisfactions of its pursuit and mastery.

≈ Veteran teachers, practiced in their ways and classroom characters, who may need reassurance about the value, indeed sometimes the glory, of their efforts, and who may also seek the inspiration and encouragement to evaluate their old habits and to consider new ones.

≈ Those many people—parents, students, administrators, members of governing boards, and public officials—who evaluate teaching for personal or professional reasons.

≈ And those many others who, with no less seriousness of intent or moral concern than professional teachers, occasionally instruct other people in unfamiliar tasks—parents, police officers, managers, counselors, coaches, and all professionals—in fact, anyone and everyone.

The book originates in our personal experiences. It represents the distillation of two lifetimes of teaching in many settings, from an elementary school classroom in the slums of southeast London to graduate seminars in an Ivy League university. Yet it is in no sense a memoir; it contains no references to personal history. It is instead, as Gilbert Highet characterized his own penetrating *Art of Teaching*, "a book of suggestions drawn from practice."

Because the book is intended to highlight the qualities that make up great teaching, we have thought it useful to illustrate the form and shape which these qualities may take in classrooms with the portraits of teachers—good and bad, exemplary and cautionary—at work. While the characters are fictional, they are by no means figments of our fancy; we have drawn their traits and tactics from teachers we have known and from our own experiences. We wish the sketches to demonstrate teaching in progress—a living process full of teachers' faults, foibles, mistakes, quirks, fancies, and blemishes as well as their virtues and triumphs. No single person to our knowledge has ever possessed all the virtues or vices we portray, but all these attributes of teachers have existed somewhere, sometime. By illustrating with concrete examples the general elements of which we have written, we hope to help make somewhat abstract qualities come to life.

Every idea in this book rests on our conviction that, for those who pursue it seriously, teaching is a calling, a summons from within; that it is among life's noblest and most responsible activities—an activity in which we have all engaged at one time or another as parents, workers, and friends; and that those who teach with fullness of heart and complete engagement are entitled to every honor and support that their communities can extend. Thus we hope to find as readers those who wish to understand, as we have tried to understand, good teaching wherever and however it occurs. We have written for all, like ourselves, who would gladly learn that gladly they might (better) teach.

The book has been greatly improved by the engaged readings and wise reflections of those who have exercised their critical powers on earlier versions of the manuscript: Olivia P. Banner, Christine R. Beacham, Paul L. Brannan, Betty M. Cannon, Edwin J. Delattre, A. Graham Down, Richard Ekman, Barbara C. Follansbee, Alan Fraker, Dennis Gray, Norman Hirschfeld, Phyllis Hirschkop, Marvin Hirshfeld, Gwin J. Kolb,

Bryce V. Lambert, Jacob Neusner, Roger Rosenblatt, Robert A. Scott, Eileen Sheehy, and Jane Zacek—teachers all! Mark Carroll and Dana J. Pratt provided sage advice and comforting assurance about the publication of the work. At Yale University Press, Dan Heaton's editorial gifts greatly sharpened the text, and Charles Grench warmly encouraged and skillfully supported our work. While relieving them all of responsibility for any errors that may remain and for all arguments with which they may still disagree, we are nevertheless deeply grateful for their assistance and counsel.

The Elements of Teaching

✑ *Introduction*

MOST TEACHERS forget that teaching is an art. Trained in the sciences and techniques of education, professional teachers are conscientious in applying the psychology and methods that they have learned. They may not call what they are trying to do "teaching" and may prefer instead such terms as *explanation, instruction, demonstration, guidance,* or simply *setting a good example.* Yet even those who have enjoyed first-class professional preparation, when summoned to instruct, guide, and inform those entrusted to them, are faced with one of the greatest, because earliest, challenges of teaching: they must improvise as best they can. And they rarely get it right the first time. Only after much repetition, some nervous invention, occasional losses of temper, and general frustration, do their own processes of learning lurch forward. Then they lick their wounds, and, perhaps wondering why they were ever willing to try to teach anyone anything in the first place, they gradually perfect their art. Some teachers, whether professional or amateur, may never manage to get it right; some may fail to teach anyone anything important at all. Even those many of us who teach more or less effectively are often overwhelmed by justifiable concern for our lesson plans and their implementation, by getting our students through our courses, and by negotiating the politics and administrative obligations that seem inherent in any calling as burdened with responsibilities as teaching. Consequently, we often simply fail to give sustained and collegial thought to teaching's broader components.

This may be because we prepare for our calling by learning the subjects we will teach and the methods by which we will teach them. And there is nothing wrong with that. Yet rarely, if ever, are we led to reflect on those dimensions of character and mind that are at the very core of what we do—which is to help others acquire both the knowledge by which they can understand life in all its fullness and the dispositions by which they can live such a life. These dimensions of our own selves constitute the core of our teaching; when we teach, we animate inert knowledge with qualities of our own personality and spirit that affect, or ought to affect, our students. Nevertheless, though these qualities differ from subjects and techniques, we rarely consider these aspects of our selves separately; rarely do we take them to be distinct from the hows and whats of instruction, which, extrinsic to ourselves and usually taught to us as we prepare to teach others, do not arise from within.

The basic elements of teaching, by contrast, are qualities that come to inhere in us, even if we do not recognize them as such or fully develop them. Rarely can they be taught. They are ingredients of our own humanity, to which contents and methods are adjunct. We must draw them from ourselves, identify, develop, and then apply them. We may know our subjects and perfect our techniques for teaching them without recognizing that, for our mastery to make a difference to our students, we must also summon from within certain qualities of personality that have little to do with subject matter or theories of instruction. We don't learn these qualities, we call them forth—and, by understanding them, we use them for the benefit of others.

While pedagogical expertise and technical knowledge are essential to it, ultimately teaching is a creative act; it makes something fresh from existing knowledge in spontaneous, improvised efforts of mind and spirit, disciplined by education and experience. Thus, unlike a technology, in which correct application produces predictable and uniform results, teaching can yield infinite surprises—infinite delights—from one moment to the next. What method can supply to teaching we know or can learn; what art can furnish out of our own selves we must imagine—and then practice.

So while we cannot predict the outcome of teaching from its ingredients, we can isolate these ingredients, much as we can those of any art, in order to examine and understand them. What ground, medium, color, form, and implements are to the visual arts, so certain constituents—learning, authority, ethics, order, imagination, compassion, patience, tenacity, character, and pleasure—are to teaching. Just as all artists learn, know, select, and employ varieties of each of the constituent elements of their craft in creating their distinct works, so teachers use the components of their own art to teach in ways as distinctive as each teacher is unique. For this reason, teaching has always defied strict and agreed-upon definition. We think we know great teaching when we encounter it, yet we find it impossible to say precisely what has gone into making it great.

We generally suppose that great artists are aware of what they are doing, of how the materials they use create the effect they strive to achieve. We imagine that they are calling forth qualities in themselves to fashion something that has never been seen or heard before. Similarly, all teachers draw upon what they are and what they know when they try to advance the knowledge of their students. While teaching shares some of the attributes of science—its necessary components can be identified, some of its good results can be repeated, discoveries about it can be built upon—it is intrinsically an imaginative synthesis. It is the making of something new out of barely organized components. Its aim, especially with young students, is to fill and enlarge the character and spirit, as well as the mind, of others. And like every art, it is composed of acts of faith—endeavors of hope that our efforts to extend knowledge in others will somehow "take" with them.

Teachers differ from artists, however, in that they are rarely invited, as they pursue their calling, to think about what they are and what they know of themselves, although some of them eventually find ways to do so. For most teachers, consideration of the elements that make up their daily work—the ingredients out of which they compose their art—forms part neither of their professional preparation nor of their subsequent continuing education. And teachers at all levels spend very little professional time discussing these matters with colleagues.

This is a serious loss to teachers and, more critically, to their students. For if teachers are trustees of their students' welfare, they must consider not just why they are teaching and how, but also with what. That is to say, they must know what their acts exemplify, what qualities of life and character they themselves embody, as they try to convey knowledge to others.

These qualities of life and character constitute teaching wherever it takes place, not just in classrooms. What applies to teaching there applies equally to teaching in the wider world outside—to all of those who teach anything to anyone. It is nevertheless in classrooms that teaching is meant to be sustained and continuous. It is from teaching there that so many teachers draw most of their income; it is there that they satisfy their consuming professional engagement and guard the welfare of others, mostly younger and more vulnerable than themselves. The elements of teaching are employed with greater concentration and embodied with greater consequence in classrooms than anywhere else.

The qualities of character and mind desirable in all teachers are not, however, handed to us like the Ten Commandments; neither their number nor their nature is fixed in stone. Yet some of those qualities are more important in teaching than others. Without these central qualities, any act of teaching is incomplete. One can no more teach without learning, imagination, and compassion than one can be a cleric without faith or a sculptor without vision. But even more, the main elements of teaching do not exist merely as components of the art of teaching; they also convey what they embody—such as order, patience, and character—directly to others by the very fact of what they are. Teachers are ethical not only because the trusteeship role of instruction requires it; teachers are ethical so that their students can learn how to be ethical, too. Teachers exhibit pleasure in the classroom not only to enhance learning but also to exhibit to their students the delight that comes with acquiring and using knowledge.

The principal elements of teaching are therefore ways of transmitting certain desirable qualities of human character, as well as knowledge, to students. Because teachers are responsible for passing on to others many positive human traits through their embodiment of them, teaching is not for the fainthearted, nor for those who consider it just a means of diffusing knowledge. It requires a fullness of self, braced by consciousness of the effect each teacher has or ought to have on students, and this breadth of character is demanded of few, if any, other callings. While learning requires much effort, teaching entails an even greater one because it is more laden with moral and human responsibilities.

Yet despite its difficulties, as we know from countless experiences of our own, both as students and as instructors, teachers attain extraordinary victories over ignorance each day. How does this happen? Occasionally by virtue of nature's gifts. But more often it comes about from practice over time. One does not start out teaching in possession of all the fully developed qualities of a fine teacher. With experience and self-knowledge, however, these qualities grow and ripen; and after having felt intimidated by the demands of teaching and often discouraged by the dimensions and responsibilities of the work, one can come close to mastering its challenges and become a teacher in the fullest sense of the word.

Thus although what follows alludes frequently to the demands of teaching and emphasizes why teaching is so deeply freighted with moral responsibilities, it should also suggest why teaching can be so exhilarating and its successes are such great achievements of human endeavor.

ᕯ Learning

ALL TEACHING involves the transmission of knowledge, like the handing-on of the torch in the Olympic Games. Just as the flame must stay alive while the torch passes from hand to hand, so knowledge must remain kindled if anything is to be transferred from teacher to student. If the fire of knowledge is extinguished in teachers, even the best students are unlikely to reignite the torch and carry it to its ultimate destination—the achievement of understanding.

Teachers are presumed to possess knowledge, which their teaching communicates to their students. It follows that in order to teach they must know what they teach and know how to teach it; and in order to teach effectively, they must know deeply and well. Teaching requires more than knowing how to learn, although that is important. Above all, teaching requires learning itself; and, if possible under the demanding conditions that face so many teachers, it requires mastery of a subject.

By *learning* we usually mean one or all of three things: the act of gaining knowledge—"to learn something"—the knowledge gained by virtue of that act—"that which is known"—and the process of gaining knowledge—"learning how." All three are essential to good teaching. And each kind of learning is and must be a lifelong pursuit, not something that, as is so often mistakenly believed, fills only the years before teachers enter their classrooms. True teachers always seek (often they must struggle) to learn more, to remain current with what is known about their subjects, to keep those subjects fresh and exciting enough to sustain the exhausting act of teaching day in and day out, year after year—in sum, to expand their ability to teach. The need to keep learning has to do also with the nature of knowledge itself. Often thought to be static, knowledge is ever-changing and ever-growing; the known is never the same from one day to the next. Thus to possess and master knowledge, one must wrestle with it constantly, fashioning and refashioning what one knows and how to present it. Knowledge taunts us with its difficulty, its incompleteness, its ambiguity. As Aeschylus reminds us in the *Agamemnon*, to learn is to suffer.

Yet many mistakenly believe that teachers, at least at the pre-collegiate levels, can get by without learning, that they can just step into the classroom after gaining the minimum amount of knowledge in order to justify their being paid while they pursue their real love—say, coaching football—from which they cannot otherwise earn a living. But students know better, as the many jokes about coaches in the classroom and ill-prepared teachers attest. Students usually know which of their teachers think teaching a mere job and which of them approach it as a learned calling. The most ambitious students quickly spot the teacher without command of a subject or the one who has no genuine thirst for knowledge; they mark that teacher as lacking in authority, as someone whose ignorance of a subject poses a threat to their own well-being by preventing them from learning all they might be taught. And they are right, for their well-being as students depends on their teachers' knowledge, and on their teachers' willingness to learn more all the time.

By saying that the true teacher must master a body of knowledge, we distinguish knowledge from information. Much confusion results from mistaking one for the other. Information is to knowledge what sound is to music, the unorganized material out of which the structured result is composed. We do not ask teachers to convey information; we seek information from newspapers or price tags on items in a store. Instead, we ask teachers to transmit knowledge, that which is organized and formally known about a subject—facts, findings, explanations, hypotheses, and theories accepted for their proven accuracy, significance, beauty, utility, or power.

The struggle to gain and sustain this knowledge is probably the most exacting work of any teacher, and it never ends. True mastery of any subject is probably beyond our reach, but reach we must. Sustained intellectual vitality requires a self-imposed sentence to hard labor—the kind of labor, however, that liberates rather than imprisons, with all the satisfactions and rewards of liberation.

No one should think that mastery of a body of knowledge is easy. It is devilishly difficult, necessitating a degree of devotion, concentration, discipline, and effort demanded by few other pursuits. And because knowledge is always a work in progress, it is never complete; we must run to keep up with it.

Mastering a body of knowledge well enough to convey it to others is a lonely task; it is usually a silent conversation between someone who is learning and others—authors, scientists, artists —many of whom are dead, known only through their words on the page; the symbols with which they have worked, or the art they have created. Often, too, learning must proceed without external incentives or rewards—no additional pay, no more promotions. Gaining knowledge is private, individual, solitary. How then is knowledge sustained? And why should it be?

For the most skilled and devoted teachers, knowledge comes through an intense love of learning and of a subject, a love whose origins may be mysterious and unknown, awakened perhaps by a chance encounter with a children's book, by a parent's praise, or by a cherished teacher's encouragement—by something special that forever marked the future teacher. Most devoted teachers were "hooked" early by some distinctive curiosity, whose magic and mystery continues to hold them; and thus the best teachers must always try similarly to "hook" their own students. Knowledge, to say nothing of keenness of instruction, is also sustained by a never-ceasing aspiration to learn more, an insatiable yearning to know and to understand. So, too, knowledge is strengthened by teachers' openness to students' beguiling ability to involve them in their own learning, to pull teachers in with their own excitement and curiosity.

So teachers are and must be thinkers in their own right, not just doers who happen to teach and possess the skill to do so. Their minds must be continually restocked and nourished. They must become capable of gaining and using knowledge on their own, independent of others, and of leading others to do so, too. True teachers liberate the thinking of others.

What, then, does it mean to say that a teacher must possess learning?

Learning means knowing and mastering a subject. For many people, thrust suddenly into a new classroom and asked suddenly to teach a new subject, this may seem an impossible luxury. Yet a teacher must seek to have full command of a subject, not just enough knowledge to get by or to know more than the very best students. A teacher should possess enough knowledge of a subject to be able to consider it independently, to play confidently with it, to entertain surmises about it, to imagine its possible significances and implications when it is placed in various contexts. A teacher, that is, should know enough to be a thinker as well as an instructor. When that is the case, the teacher has joined a discipline, a professional guild of people with an agreed-upon warrant to consider themselves guardians of, and contributors to, a branch of knowledge.

Learning embodies the act of learning. In many respects, the search for knowledge is infectious; it can be transmitted to others, and it can be caught. Possibly the best way for teachers to transmit learning is to embody the act of doing so—to be seen among papers and books ("these kinsmen of the shelf," as Emily Dickinson called them), scurrying toward a library, exclaiming upon the solution to a problem, expressing delight when a student proposes a plausible interpretation new to the teacher. Teachers, in showing their students how to learn, must seek to be caught *flagrante delicto* with their subject, for the aspiration to learn should be as compelling to students as the knowledge they gain. It is a teacher's infectious enthusiasm for learning itself, as much as the student's own curiosity about the teacher's subject, that is apt to captivate a student.

Veteran teachers, long familiar with the material they teach, may choose to stop learning because it seems no longer justified.

This is always a mistake, if only because it risks suggesting an unbridgeable distance between the teacher, who seems to know it all, and the students, who may think they know nothing—which is also wrong. Thus for a teacher to stop learning is to destroy one of the principal means a teacher has to bridge the gap between ignorance and knowledge and between despair and hope. What is more, to stop learning suggests to students that a teacher is bored with the subject; and, alas, boredom is every bit as infectious as enthusiasm.

Learning requires keeping up with one's subject. This may be a teacher's hardest task, for it requires application after the normal, depleting workday is done. Yet it must be undertaken. If a teacher falls behind in a subject, so do the students, whose preparation for advancement in competition with others is thereby diminished. Keeping current with a body of knowledge does not, however, necessitate only solitary reading and study; it can be accomplished with colleagues in study groups, in formal programs of continuing professional education, and by attendance at meetings of scholars and fellow professionals. What matters is not the means of staying abreast of knowledge but the actual pursuit of that knowledge.

Learning conveys the spirit and love of learning to others. All teachers are in effect missionaries for their subjects. They must care passionately about what they teach; they must be able to reveal to their students how exciting learning can be. That is an additional reason why teachers must clearly possess knowledge, or at least display a visible desire to possess it; only then can their love of knowledge be exemplified in their enthusiasm and bearing, in the sheer fun of engaging in discussion, hunting down a fact, polishing a skill, exploring a new subject, reading a book for the first time. Of course, trying to transmit knowledge has its risks, the chief being that students often do not want to learn—or at least to learn what they are asked to learn at the time in their lives when they are asked to learn it. A pertinent story is told of John Scotus Erigena, an Irish teacher and philosopher in the court of the Holy Roman Emperor in northern France. Our philosopher was murdered by a group of his students who hacked him to death with their pens because, it is said, he tried to force them to think.

One moral of this tale, among others, is that not all subjects, after all, captivate students as naturally as, say, learning to drive attracts the interest of teenagers. The culture has already done a reasonably good job of explaining to the young the advantages of driving a car. But when it comes to such subjects as foreign languages or the physical sciences, teachers have more work cut out for them; it is they, and few others, who can best reveal how and why subjects scarcely known to their students offer excitement, satisfaction, and utility. And to do that, teachers must know their subjects thoroughly and assume the responsibility and risk of finding ways to impart those subjects to their often recalcitrant students.

Learning means being open to the knowledge of others, especially of one's own students. Often, because teachers must learn from other authorities in a field, they forget that their students may be authorities too, that they may surpass their teachers in love for a subject, or knowledge of it, or skill and intelligence. After all, is it not all teachers' best dream that their students become so fueled by their teachers' knowledge as to surpass it? Thus teachers must signal to their students that the search for knowledge is cooperative and collective, that its pursuit is a shared journey—though one that often requires much solitary work.

Detecting ignorance while inadvertently overlooking understanding is one of the great hazards of all teaching. That is why teachers must work hard to encourage their students to make known their knowledge to other students; that is why they must provide the settings, free from constraint and evaluation, in which students can do so. In this way, teachers themselves are helped to focus on what students know rather than on what they do not.

Learning provides the basis for independent thought. Active engagement in a field of knowledge becomes critical at that stage when teachers realize that their engagement arises from the possession of enough knowledge to be confident in thinking about the field independently. Recognition of oneself as a thinker as well as a teacher—as someone who is part of a larger community of learning, as capable as anyone else of engaging in the intellectual play of knowledge—may be among the most difficult transitions in a teacher's professional life. Yet when that transition occurs, a new world opens, new authority is gained, and a new teacher is born—one who determines independently what is best for students and what they should know. At this stage, too, the teacher recognizes that learning is an end in itself, that not everything needs to be related to instruction, that thinking is a world without end, without known outcome.

Learning justifies learning. A teacher's confidence in the intrinsic worth of knowledge is fundamental to all instruction. Such deep-rooted belief makes a teacher able to relate knowledge to life, to all human experience. To students' typical questions, "Why do we have to learn this? What good is such knowledge?" the typical instrumental answers come to mind easily: "Because it's required by the school board." "Because you will do better on your licensing exam." "Because you'll need it later when you study economics." But the teacher with deep learning answers with conviction and authority more pertinently: "Because acquiring this knowledge is difficult. Because you will feel triumphant when it no longer confuses you. Because you will enjoy what you can do with it. Because in learning it you may discover new perspectives on life, new ways of thinking. Because its possession will make you more alive than its alternative, which is ignorance."

The teachers whom we remember most vividly are those who knew their subjects best and transmitted them with the greatest intensity and love. They were confident in their knowledge, and not dogmatic; they acted out their own struggles to understand in front of us, joyful when they understood something fresh, troubled when they did not or could not know. They joined us at the laboratory bench, in the library, at the museum, puzzling with us over a test tube result, complaining about a book's interpretation, discovering a painting's meaning. They stood before us to present the act of learning with a sort of honesty that we rarely encounter in everyday life. It is such examples of passion and exhilaration that students need in their teachers. Only in that way can students meet the importunate demands of learning with a full heart; only then can the thirst for learning move them on.

⤝⤝⤝

FELICIA GONZALEZ tucked her two children into bed, told them each a favorite bedtime story, kissed them good night, and returned to the kitchen. With her husband away on business, it fell to her to clean up from dinner and straighten up the children's toys alone. It was 9 o'clock; she'd be up at 6, getting her children off to school at 7:30, and in front of her first class at 8:30. Fortunately, she had no papers to grade, and earlier that afternoon she had reviewed what she was going to teach tomorrow by skimming through class preparation notes from the past few times she had taught the same course. So she could go to bed. Yet she hadn't opened the new book that she'd bought on the establishment clause of the Constitution, and she would be teaching about the First Amendment to her eleventh-grade advanced placement history class the next day. She realized that she should try to read some of the new work. And so she did— not to her satisfaction, but enough to learn its author's argument and to reexamine what the Framers meant by an establishment of religion. She turned off the light at 11.

The next day, sure enough, one of her students asked her to explain not the clauses prohibiting limits on the right of assembly or of the press, which were the usual subjects of discussion, but the meaning of an establishment of religion. But those two hours with the new book had not helped her very much. While informed enough about the meaning of an establishment, Ms. Gonzalez could not yet explain its historical complexities—the eighteenth-century position of the Church of England in the colonies, the existence of multiple establishments ("How could there have been lots of established churches in a single state?" one student pressed her. "If that was so, why were the Framers so worried?"), and so on. She left school that day dissatisfied with herself.

She decided to turn her frustration (and, she admitted to herself, her embarrassment) into a shared effort: she and her students would study together so that she, as well as they, could get the answers she sought. So she devised a paper assignment in which each original state had its own single student historian; the Bill of Rights got three students and the Church of England one; and she decided to take James Madison for herself. For the next month, she frequently joined her students in the school and town libraries, studied Madison's "Memorial and Remonstrance," and steeped herself in his writings about the Virginia Statute of Religious Freedom and the Bill of Rights. When her students' papers were due, she had her own paper ready for them to read, just as they read each other's and she all of theirs. Of course, her students were somewhat uneasy about reading hers—especially when she asked them to comment on it and give her a grade. (An A, they decided, even though she had misspelled the name of Madison's birthplace.)

The class got so involved in the subject that some of its members decided to enter the state's National History Day competition. Spending afternoons with them, Ms. Gonzalez helped them plan and design a display that, after competing for the contest, could travel to libraries throughout the county. When the project won, she took the whole class out for ice cream. When the project competed in the national competition, it won first place there, too. She was so proud of her students that she decided that they needed more than ice cream this time; she wanted recognition for them.

Usually, the large display board in front of the high school carried only sports news, like "Cavaliers 8–0 for Season. Conference Champs." She wanted a change.

The principal was reluctant: "What will the community think? It's only interested in the teams."

"Well," she replied, "Let's try to change its ways. Let's recognize the students who achieve by learning."

For the rest of the year, all those who rode by could read "Cavaliers Win National History Day Championship. School Has Five Merit Scholarship Finalists."

Spurred by the success of her assignment on religious establishments and by her students' success in their National History Day contests, Ms. Gonzalez tried something she had long contemplated but, fearing parental objections, had never dared. She wished to get away from the brief and denatured treatment of religion in the required textbook and transform it so that her students could learn in greater depth about this central engine of American history. Moreover, she hoped to have her students study religion throughout the course, not just when studying disestablishment or the great revivals of the nineteenth century.

So seeing her opportunity in the group of students she chanced to have this year, she seized it. Her desire to continue treating religion as integral to American history, to include the subject throughout the advanced placement syllabus in future courses, however, would demand much of her—more study, more preparations—and all on her own, for the summer institute on American religions that she had applied for was not scheduled for six months. Yet she was determined to teach what she wanted most to learn about; and she was determined to do so in a way that taught about religion while avoiding any hint of indoctrination.

When she dug in, she discovered that the self-imposed task was almost too much for her. Her family found her devoting more time than usual to reading and studying in what free time she had. Nevertheless, she was determined to add the study of religion, a subject she had long thought missing, to her course. To help divide the labor, she assigned separate religions to each student—Free Will Baptism to a Jew, Judaism to a Catholic, Mormonism to an African-American Muslim, Pentecostalism to an atheist, and so on, so as to expose each to new perspectives and to broaden the knowledge of each. Lacking an appropriate text that she could assign, she had to undertake much more lecturing than she liked. But if she did not become the authority and provide guidance, who else would? To questions from colleagues about the danger of proselytizing, she had a ready answer: "I won't tolerate it. Yet this course is not going to be about religious appreciation—everyone learning a little bit about lots of creeds. Each student is going to learn about one religion in some depth. The students can't understand the nation's history without understanding its people's religious faiths and the elements of them that permeate all our culture."

Ms. Gonzalez's curiosity inspired her students to become curious, too. By the end of the course, a couple of her Jewish students knew more about their own faith for having studied the struggles of German and Irish Catholics to protect their immigrant religions in a predominantly Protestant nation. One self-styled atheist had become deeply knowledgeable about Jehovah's Witnesses. The last day of class, her very best student expressed admiration for how much Ms. Gonzalez knew about American history.

"Well," she replied obliquely, "we've all had to work hard, haven't we?"

"We sure have," the student replied. "And some of us have been wondering what your own religious faith is."

"I didn't want you to know while we were considering religion in general and the many religious faiths represented in the United States," she said. "But there's no harm in your knowing now. I'm a Methodist. But in the classroom, I've tried to express another faith—the faith that we can all learn a lot together. I hope that I've done so, and I hope that you're converted to that faith."

✎ Authority

DISCUSSIONS OF TEACHING seldom include any mention of authority. Yet we cannot teach without it. It is at the center of all our efforts in the classroom, the workshop, and the office. A teacher's instruction may lack many of the other useful elements of instruction and still have some beneficial effect, but teaching without authority ceases to be teaching at all. If teachers have no command of their classrooms, their students ignore their knowledge, and their compassion for their students' efforts is pointless. Yet what is authority, and why is it so important to teaching?

Authority in teaching, as in anything else, is legitimate influence over others. It is not mere power. It differs from power in its moral component and because, while power may be used for good or ill, authority does not connote coercion. Authority has the unusual quality of being dual, or reciprocal, and thus dependent upon others for its fulfillment; in the classroom, it is composed both of a teacher's knowledge, character, and conduct and of students' respect given back to the teacher in free acknowledgement of the teacher's greater understanding of the subject at hand and greater ability to convey it. Power, on the other hand, is coercive force—the exertion of will to command action—whose basis is dependency and often fear. As such, power has no place in teaching; its use is contrary to students' interests.

The distinction between power and authority in a teacher is crucial to understanding the true nature of teaching. In the classroom as elsewhere, one may have power without the authority to exercise it; such power without authority is little more than force. But authority can exist without power because of its moral nature, because of its relationship to equity, empathy, and truth. Authority is thus an attribute that a teacher gains, if only indirectly, by deserving it; it is an aspect of personal character. When students have long forgotten much of the subject a teacher has taught, they will remember and perhaps reflect the teacher's bearing toward knowledge and life.

Much confusion exists about the origins and nature of teachers' authority. Many teachers—being employees of some public agency, such as a school board or a public university—are technically civil officers. Consequently, their authority may legally originate in the official source of their employment, and their responsibility may seem to consist in their strict fidelity to community norms, rather than in other equally or more insistent claims, such as to their students' welfare. Teachers' authority over their students is also limited by the involvement of families and the state in students' lives; whether they like it or not, teachers share responsibility with others who may intervene in students' behalf for their well-being.

In addition, teachers' authority cannot arise, as does that of other professionals, from the independence of expert and client, each of whom may leave the other. Like physicians toward their patients and attorneys toward their clients, teachers are bound to prescribe, on the basis of their knowledge and experience, what is in their students' best interests; they must teach students what they believe students must know, not what students may wish to know. But unlike medical patients and legal clients, students cannot readily refuse a teacher's advice or, at least in primary and secondary schools in most places, legally leave school; students are their instructors' captives, at least for a time. It is this dependence of students that places special obligations upon their teachers.

Moreover, teachers are custodians of culture. They are responsible for passing on and helping students to absorb and learn to evaluate the beliefs and traditions of the society of which they are members. Though teachers share this task with others, they are charged by the community with special responsibility for instilling the skills (such as literacy), knowledge, intellectual powers, and norms that the community itself holds most important. It is therefore their particular obligation both to help convey tradition and history to their students and to assess the validity of customs and community norms with dispassion, sympathy, and understanding. In return for expecting the community to give them some leeway in accomplishing this delicate task, teachers must be mindful that their authority to do so hinges in part upon the seriousness, the balance, and, above all, the knowledge they bring to it.

Because of this, while teachers have a profound responsibility for students' intellectual and moral nurture, as well as responsibility toward the society and culture of which the students are part, they have this responsibility without the full liberties and independence of other professionals. Often, they are not free to teach anything they want in the manner they think is in their students' best interests. This lack of complete freedom makes the preservation of their authority so important; their authority rests primarily on their own qualities as a person—on their thoughtfulness, dignity, and knowledge—not on their professional independence.

What, then, can teachers do to gain, foster, deserve, and sustain their authority?

Authority requires a climate for serious learning. It does not depend on controlling a classroom or making students behave, although both may result from authority born of teachers' learning, stature, and behavior. Rather, authority grows from a moral bearing toward knowledge, from *gravitas*—actions and words that convey teachers' inner convictions about the worth and use of knowledge, as well as the determination to impart what they know and a willingness to admit to their own ignorance or doubt. A teacher cannot flaunt authority or insist upon it. If it is forced, students sense immediately its origins in insecurity, its inauthenticity—that is, the absence of the sense of self that underlies all genuine authority.

Instead, teachers' authority must arise from the seriousness of purpose they convey to their students—a seriousness that can be conveyed as much through laughter as through gravity. But it must in all cases be linked to students' own well-being in such a way that they are drawn to knowledge, not forced to swallow it. For instance, it is probably better to try to attract students to chemistry by expressing the hope that they will find it fascinating and useful rather than by insisting on the importance of chemistry and the necessity of learning it.

Authority means mastery of a subject. A natural gift of physical stature or a distinctive voice may confer some measure of authority on some people. But for most teachers, substantial knowledge of the subjects they teach is the foundation of their stature. Those who have full command of their subjects are able to present them in a variety of aspects and forms and can distinguish what their students know and what they do not. These teachers can modify their approaches to their subjects according to the differences in each group of students. They are able to use their students' questions and uncertainties as launching pads for further inquiry and discussion. This means that they can present a variety of viewpoints where interpretation is called for, without indicating to students which one is their own—a matter of great ethical importance.

Mastery does not mean that a teacher knows so much about a subject that there is nothing further to learn about it, for learning is always an endless journey. Instead, mastery should mean that good teachers are those who have made good progress in that journey, are willing to retrace their steps along it, and thus can help those behind them find their own way on the same path.

Authority is a matter of carriage and conduct as well as knowledge. It springs as much from bearing as from study and reflection. Teachers may gain respect, for instance, by dress and speech—by, say, greater care of attire and greater accuracy of expression. Yet more important in establishing authority are those attributes of personal character and citizenship— like dignity and civility, compassion and fairness—by which students may be better able to guide themselves. Teachers must try to represent and exhibit those qualities that they want their students to develop (and that their students are aware they are expected to develop). Finally, a teacher's authority, because it is also a manifestation of character, grows from knowledge of and confidence in one's self. As a teacher learns to reach inward for the wisdom of which knowledge and experience are the essential elements, then authority becomes natural and irresistible to students.

Authority is acquired and accumulated. It is rarely innate. In this regard, the creation and preservation of authority is much like the mastery of knowledge: it calls for unremitting effort. Teachers gain authority in the classroom through practice and experience, by thinking hard about authority's nature and use, by experimentation, and above all by their advancing self-knowledge. Although this process of learning extends over a long period, teachers must lose no chance to possess and deserve authority; they must strive to establish it immediately, from the first moment of a class, and to evince those qualities of character that make students look to them for understanding and guidance. And while young or fledgling teachers should not be expected to possess the authority of seasoned instructors, even they must be able to indicate from the first that they know how to lead their students so that it is exciting and rewarding to follow them. Fortunately, they often have the enthusiasm and energy that age may lack, and those qualities can compensate for an initial insufficiency of professional experience and maturity.

Authority encourages aspiration in students. Authority must have direction; it must be linked to purpose; it does not exist for itself. A teacher's authority must be devoted to helping students strengthen their accustomed capacities and reach beyond their habitual ways. A teacher's dedication must not be directed only to students' understanding of the world, nor just to the deepening of their moral life. Authority in a teacher creates the desire in students to surpass themselves; and this desire can endure far beyond the classroom as students develop the habit of trying always to "stretch"—be it in their accumulation of knowledge, in their contributions to public life, or in their moral sensibility. Great teachers and great schools are distinguished in large part from average teachers and average schools by the strength and longevity of ambition they instill in their students.

Authority requires some formal distance between teachers and students. Because teachers' authority grows from the implicit acknowledgement of their greater knowledge of a subject and deeper understanding of their students' welfare than is possessed by the students themselves, teachers are usually better able to assist their students in gaining more knowledge and attaining greater maturity than are the students' friends and contemporaries. However deeply committed to students' welfare teachers must be, one of the quickest ways for teachers to dissipate their authority is to act as their students' "pals." Popularity is not authority, nor is teaching a popularity contest. Authority stems in part from students' understanding that a teacher maintains strict impartiality among them and ostensibly has no favorites. In that way the teacher's awarding of grades and otherwise assessing students' performance and growth are accepted by students as legitimate.

Teachers may be students' instructors, advisers, confessors, audiences, cheerleaders, even idols; such mentors may, indeed should, show compassion and empathy, reveal the pleasures of sharing learning with younger people, and extend warmth and friendly affection. But teachers should never be students' close friends or companions, never their intimates. Teachers must act as adults, not youths; this requires that teachers bear themselves as knowing more, as being better prepared to understand what is best for their students' welfare, and as possessing the equanimity and serenity that most young people have not yet acquired. And because they must be prepared to evaluate, grade, direct, reprove, and sometimes discipline their students, they must have the authority to stand back and be objective in their estimation of each student's efforts and achievements while not losing their students' respect for their authority to do so.

Authority emerges from an acknowledged difference in the status of teacher and student. Distance, detachment, and impartiality are meant to maintain what some find difficult to accept but which nevertheless remains a major source of authority—an acknowledged superiority in a teacher's status. That superior status, however, does not owe itself to teachers' responsibilities for grading their students or to their right to correct students. Rather, that status is gained due to teachers' superiority of knowledge and greater experience. Teachers are not necessarily superior people, nor are they expected to have superior athletic skills, or to be better spouses, or to have greater insight into national affairs than their students. They are, however, expected to know more. Greater knowledge of a subject and greater skill in conveying it are what distinguishes teachers not only from students but from parents and school board members and other professionals.

While both a larger store of knowledge and better behavior imply superiority, in fact they necessitate humility; they manifest themselves indirectly. Teachers who can lead their classes to experience pleasure in, for example, understanding the juncture of religion, engineering, and aesthetics in the construction of a Gothic cathedral gain authority through this process of making learning satisfying. Teachers who can take potentially confrontational classroom situations and lead their students instead to listen to their classmates' radically different views and respond with patient consideration will be recognized by their students for their higher sense of fairness.

Yet paradoxically, a teacher can also gain authority by denying it—that is, by acknowledging ignorance. The simple "I don't know, and I wish I did," or "I can't answer that question, and I wish I could" are clarifying through their direct honesty—and imply a yearning to know. Mastery of a subject neither requires nor implies omniscience. Admitting ignorance may risk both reducing the precious distance between teacher and students and exposing to question the teacher's superiority of learning and experience. Yet by confessing ignorance, a teacher creates an opportunity to explore a subject further, to reach for or ask a student to reach for a book that will provide the answer, to discuss with students how the answer might be found, or to design an assignment by which students singly or collectively can try to find out. Thus "I don't know" becomes "Let's look it up" (a lesson in research) or "Let's find out together" (a lesson in experiment and cooperation). In these ways, knowledge has a chance to emerge from ignorance, truth from error, method from confusion, and understanding from puzzlement.

We say that ethical actions, character, and imagination are basic elements of teaching. Authority, we say, is gained. Of all the qualities of great teachers, only authority must be earned; it is the only quality dependent upon others' estimation of us and of the qualities of mind and character that we possess as teachers. Yet authority's very dependence upon the views of those we teach gives it its peculiar strength once earned, for it embraces students as accessories in its existence, placing upon them responsibilities for the atmosphere in which their own learning takes place. This mutuality of responsibility for its existence confers distinctiveness on authority and makes it, of all the elements of teaching, both the most fragile and, once possessed, the most commanding. No other requires greater care in its creation; no other opens greater doors to learning in its use.

About Jasper Stampa there was nothing prepossessing. Standing five feet five, his arms too long for his body's proportions, his face half-framed by an ill-kempt graying beard, he was usually overlooked in a roomful of people, even in one filled by his colleagues. Those who knew him as a friend— and there were not many—reported that he collected Romanian military decorations, though they could not say why; and his students, to whom he would occasionally, if shyly, confide something personal, laughed at the news that he and his family had vacationed in Albany.

Yet Professor Stampa's forgettable looks and curious ways belied his reputation. There were a few things about this strange little man that drew students to him. It was known on campus that he was deadly serious about his own scholarship—on composers' changing use of the hemidemisemiquaver—and that he was respected elsewhere for it. He continued to wear a coat and tie when other members of the faculty had begun to sport jeans and long after dress codes for collegians had been given up as hopelessly retrograde. (To those who expressed surprise at this single mark of quaint fastidiousness, he explained, conveying his own puzzlement at their interest, that, after all, he was of a different age and time than his students; "and, anyway, who would want to dress like them?") It was also known that, while he was a "hard marker," he was also fair to his students and made his expectations clear.

This shambling man, once in the classroom, came alive and even seemed to grow taller when standing before his students. On the opening day of his course on the history of music (a distribution requirement, which many students assumed would be easy and fun), he would enter precisely at the class's appointed hour, walk with uncharacteristic briskness to the lectern, wait gravely for stragglers to enter, then remark quietly that, because music was so wonderful and its history so fascinating, all were expected to be in their seats on time. "That's when we start listening so we can learn. Latecomers disturb others and miss what others have already heard. I'd prefer," and here he'd frown, "that if you're late you don't come to class at all." And he meant it: from time to time, he would refuse entry to a late student, never failing, however, to explain again why.

On the first day he would arrive also carrying an armful of books; and, placing them down, he would announce that the course was intended to enable every course member to understand these works by faithfully completing every assignment. "But don't worry," he'd say; "your assignments are more readable and thinner. Yet by the end of the course, you'll be able to read and understand what's in these. It won't be easy; you'll have to work hard; and I have the usual incentives"—he would wave a grade book about—"to assist you to do so. But I can tell you this: If you read your assignments along with me, a whole new world will open to you. You'll learn not just to listen to music but to understand what you're hearing. And there's nothing to rival that joy—at least I know of nothing. When we finish this course at the end of the year, you'll have learned about Latin motets, Haydn's quartets, the great symphonies of Brahms, and contemporary electronic compositions. And if we have time, we'll do a little work on black spirituals and contemporary jazz." Then he'd play a tape of a Gregorian chant followed by Dave Brubeck's "Take Five" and begin to talk of rhythm and meter.

Jasper Stampa was not a scintillating lecturer. He stood still behind his lectern, told no jokes, did not even criticize other scholars. Yet his intentness and obvious love of music appealed to students. Something about this man's ability to talk on and on about his subject and to have something interesting to say in response to any question made them learn the subject, many of them in spite of themselves; he seemed to know everything about Western music and much about African and Asian as well. One year, the class's poorest student, expecting that his enrollment in Dr. Stampa's course would mean an easy time in a class that just listened to music, was heard saying that "the course was great. He made me understand how we got from that guy Monteverdi to heavy metal."

When not teaching, Professor Stampa was a picture of awkwardness and indecision. In his office he seemed to lose his tongue when asked about other courses or the rest of the curriculum. So out of touch with professional life was he that he could give his students few suggestions about graduate schools; and he would never join the faculty-student softball game in the spring. Yet when students came to talk with him about their term papers, he would come alive. Rising from his desk and drawing himself up to full height, he would climb his ladder and reach for a book (usually piled on a shelf near the ceiling) about some obscure court composer to illustrate a point about the development of Mozart's composing style. "Here," he would say. "Take this wonderful book about this mediocre musician and bring it back when you think you've figured out how Mozart graduated from that style to the magnificence of *Figaro*." And he was known to sit with a student for an hour or two playing and replaying tapes of his favorite pieces in order to help the student understand musical structure.

When Professor Stampa retired prematurely in order to complete some further research into 64th notes and move his family to Albany as permanent residents of his long-favored city, former students honored him at a banquet at which they presented him with a just-published study of atonalism, which, they admitted, was not to their taste, although they knew he loved all twentieth-century music. The book was inscribed "To Jasper Stampa, whose knowledge of music was always unbelievable and from whom we learned, through listening and reading, as he said we would, of a whole new part of art and life."

⇜ Ethics

A CHARACTER in an otherwise deservedly forgotten play by a Nazi playwright was made to remark that he had a revolver at the ready whenever he heard the word *culture*. Some are similarly inclined to draw a weapon when invited to think about ethics. The term suggests at once something old-fashioned, strait-laced, and priggish. It conjures up thoughts of a moral police, censorship, pompous rectitude, sanctimonious hypocrisy—all that is the enemy of a jealous regard for our own rights and freedom of action. Yet rightly understood, ethics implies none of these things. It has instead to do with what seems to be the natural human consideration of our moral duties and behavior toward others in a complex and imperfect world.

In teaching, ethics means putting the satisfaction of the needs and good of students before those of anyone else. This has to be so not simply because it is the right thing to do, but also because it is the surest road to students' trust and understanding and therefore the best way to ensure that they learn. Teaching thus requires student-centered ethics. If the good of our students is not the focus of our attention, they cannot be taught, and they are unlikely to learn.

For teaching is a fiduciary act. Teachers hold students' welfare in trust for the students' parents, for their larger communities, and, above all, for the students themselves. Teachers are called upon to create and secure each student's greatest good by encouraging the development of individual knowledge and understanding. This responsibility of trusteeship imbues teaching with its profound ethical significance and makes teachers not simply transmitters of knowledge but exemplars and guardians of behavior and values as well. Therefore, because the end of teaching must be the good of students, not that of teachers, the focus of teaching is quite the opposite of individualism and self-regard. The true language of teaching is that of responsibility, not rights. Teaching seeks the well-being of students, not of teachers, who must be prepared to give up something toward that end.

Of course, true self-denial comes to few of us, nor are teachers obliged to ignore themselves, their families, friends, or neighbors to devote themselves exclusively to their students. Yet in taking on the functions of teachers, they take on the duties of trusteeship. And when it comes to the trusteeship of students, especially of young ones, those responsibilities can be exacting. To fail to shoulder those responsibilities—or to fail at least to try to do so—means in effect to be not a teacher but someone who merely offers information. One of the truest tests of teachers is whether or not they welcome and bear well the ethical obligations of their work.

Like compassion and imagination, therefore, the ethical components of teaching require teachers to put themselves in their students' places, to imagine the confusions of their students and their desires to be guided toward their own good. Teachers must recall their own earlier vulnerabilities to influence, their own difficulties in learning, and their own anxieties about acceptance and popularity.

So, too, the ethics of teaching is intimately linked to the authority that teachers exercise over their students. The classroom is and must be a protected place, where students discover themselves and gain knowledge of the world, where they are free of all threats to their well-being, where all received opinion is open to evaluation, where all questions are legitimate, where the explicit goal is to see the world more openly, fully, and deeply. Teachers are therefore obliged to create and preserve an ethical climate in the classroom.

But what does it mean to be ethical in teaching?

The first rule of ethical teaching is to do no harm to students. This is not merely, in the spirit of Hippocrates' admonition to doctors, a negative injunction. Instead, it implies teachers' obligation to protect students actively from threats to their welfare arising from such appealing blandishments as popularity or peer pressure. Students' sense of self and image is easily injured by embarrassment or punishment that appears excessive, or by teachers' abuse of their authority, and this is as much the case with older as with younger students. The abuse of authority, which can take many forms, such as prejudice, favoritism, and intimacy, is especially threatening to students' welfare.

Intimacy, for example, even when it oversteps the boundaries of friendship, particularly with older students, is often said to be legitimate because it is the right of consenting adults. Such claims overlook the clear moral and professional conflicts between teachers' desires and students' good that are caused by intimacy when one intimate is called upon to evaluate objectively the performance of the other. This is to say nothing of the comparative disadvantages any intimacy may cause to those students who do not share it or are not its object. But the most serious consequence of such a breach of teachers' professional ethics is the injury it does to the trust the student has reposed in the teacher to be protector and exemplar as well as instructor. Therefore, while teachers never surrender their own legal or moral rights when they teach, in teaching others, especially the young, they take upon themselves antecedent responsibilities, akin to the responsibilities of parents for their children.

Ethical teaching requires exclusive attention to students' welfare. This may be teachers' most difficult responsibility, placing them sometimes in conflict with their own needs, hopes, and desires, as well as their obligations to others. After all, teachers are not expected to be totally selfless and to give up everything for their students. Yet the moral requirements of teaching exact from teachers an unusual degree of sacrifice, of extension of self, toward others—gifts of energy and time, and often the sacrifice of personal interest, for the benefit of their students. They are, after all, teachers' dependents, and they rely on their instructors for knowledge, guidance, and protection. Teachers are therefore obliged, as professionals, to defend their students' interests—among the chief of which is a search for the truth—against intrusion, sometimes even against school and community authorities who have it in their power to endanger teachers' employment.

Teachers also must not involve students in their own professional conflicts or allow their own actions—protracted labor strikes, for example, or participation in campus demonstrations

—to affect their obligation to their students, which is to lead them to learn. Teachers must always be engaged in envisaging for their students, and helping their students envisage for themselves, what is best for them.

Ethical teaching means setting high standards and expectations and inspiring students to meet them. Many students resist and resent challenges, and sometimes parents and communities are unsympathetic to standards that ask students to surpass themselves. But is it not the responsibility of teachers to inspire their students to "stretch" and thus to grow in knowledge and understanding—or, as one beloved teacher used to insist in one of the injunctions she would write on the blackboard each day, to "choose a high failure rather than a low success"? Like all true professionals, teachers are expected to act in their students' behalf even if the students resist taking their advice. They have to lead their students to set their own high expectations, to imagine what they may achieve, and to aspire to achieve it.

When students balk at trying harder or when they seem stuck and unable to learn more, teachers must not react by lowering their expectations. They must instead discover ways to transmit to their students their own hopes about them, to have students internalize their teachers' aspirations for them. "We won't give up," should be the motto. "I find it hard to teach about this; you don't like learning it. But we can't let you get away without learning it. So let's find another way to go at it. We're going to keep trying together."

Ethical teaching means embodying the principles of teaching. All teachers teach by example as well as by instruction; they are followed and emulated as well as understood. Students are always inclined to emulate the behavior and attitudes of those whom they see as models or who are held up to them as models, especially when those figures, the teachers, may be the adults with whom students spend the most time outside their families and who thus serve as surrogates for their parents. In fact, teachers are sometimes students' only models of good behavior and thought; always they are among young students' most significant guides to personal and occupational life. If knowledge is to be, as it must be, more than book-learning, and if other people, other institutions, fail, as they too often do, to guide students toward their own good or to offer mature examples of behavior, then teachers bear an even heavier responsibility to do what is right. Teachers must therefore exemplify mature behavior—actions, as always, speaking louder than words—and thus avoid the moral arrogance and self-righteousness that often seems to come from teaching good behavior directly.

Ethical teaching means teaching ethics. Beyond setting examples, teaching requires active efforts to teach about and instill good character. To be sure, in an age of relativism, when rival camps battle over the teaching of virtues and values, it is not easy to know how to teach ethics to students; and teachers are often confused and uncertain even about whether they should attempt to do so. But that decision is already made when they exemplify the worth and use of knowledge, service to others, or compassion. They must therefore be conscious of the moral qualities and dimensions of their work and not hesitate to teach about ethics and character.

For example, teachers must iterate and reiterate the priorities of truth, honesty, and fairness; they must instruct their students about the costs of plagiarism and cheating, including the self-injury such acts inflict upon students' developing intellect; they must apply just penalties for all breaches of ethical behavior. Teachers must also, by way of evidence amply provided in the study of history and literature (to name only the richest sources), offer instruction about good and bad, right and wrong, justice and injustice, truth and error. They must introduce their students to the sometimes agonizing ethical quandaries of life.

These lessons can be taught anywhere—in classrooms, at laboratory benches, and on the playing fields. They permeate all disciplines. To dismiss such instruction as dangerous, intrusive, or coercive is a kind of cowardice. Of course there are risks to teaching ethics and character. But if classroom work lacked such challenges, who would choose to be a teacher?

Ethical teaching means acknowledging students' minds, ways, and beliefs. Teachers must elicit from their students their own, if only faintly understood, views even while infusing in students the teachers' own more mature thinking; they must ask their students to explain their behavior and convictions, as well as lead them to explore those convictions' appropriateness and strength. While all teaching is meant to develop students' thinking by adding to their knowledge, the purpose of teaching is to enlarge, not to manipulate, their minds and spirits. What students bring to the classroom is the raw material that teaching seeks to enlarge and deepen, perhaps to refashion, but never to present as illegitimate or to obliterate. This may be teachers' most delicate task. While listening with an open heart and mind, they must try to lead their students to see and understand things afresh without injuring the better convictions and traditions the students bring to class. At the same time, however, they are bound to try to alter any baser ways and convictions they may encounter—such as violence or racism. Precisely because of their ethical freight, neither of these tasks is easy.

Classes that contain students of different racial and ethnic groups or of different ages present particular challenges. It is in such situations that the relevant experiences of students, related and discussed with care, can help others learn; and no good teacher ought to discourage such contributions when they bear on the subject being discussed.

Ethical teaching requires consideration of students' differing but tenable viewpoints. Teachers who have full command of their subjects can present them in many aspects and distinguish established facts and findings from areas of doubt and uncertainty. In fact, they must distinguish facts from fiction, hypotheses from theories, the possible from the probable, and the wise from the imprudent. Yet they must always do so with fidelity to what is known and not known; they must not offer their own opinions or beliefs as established facts or as truth. Thus in order to excite rather than suppress discussion, in order to give students' ideas full consideration, teachers must present a wide range of possible interpretations and viewpoints while scrupulously refraining from introducing their own preferences and views.

In fact, teachers cannot responsibly seek to impose their own views upon their students; to do so only inhibits the students' own thinking and discourages them from exploring new thoughts and deepening their own understanding of knowledge of proven worth. Teachers must actively encourage their students to discover and justify their own views—views that will often differ from those of their teachers and fellow students—if only as exercises in learning. It is the duty of all teachers to encourage the flowering and strengthening of their students' thoughts, not to proselytize for their own.

Yet to acknowledge students' views must not mean the avoidance of rigor or debate; teachers who let their students off easily are only patronizing them. Students should not be allowed to explain and support what is no more than their personal opinions or the expression of the way things are as solid and tested convictions or statements of proven fact; nor should they be allowed to claim as known or true what is mere opinion. Teachers must ask of their students that, among other things, they cite known evidence, employ conventional logic, and assess the relative strengths and weaknesses of each position they take; and teachers must not shrink from pointing out and explaining the relative merits and power of all arguments. Teachers' respect for their students makes itself known in the insistence that students arrive at their personal convictions only after having ventured into the struggle to test them against the world's current stock of knowledge.

The ethical dimensions of teaching, more than any others of its elements, require, like all ethical life, difficult choices between our own desires and the good of others. No one ought to minimize these difficulties or consider any of the choices teachers must make as being clear-cut. Sometimes all we can ask of ourselves is an awareness of the ethical dilemmas of our work, knowing that we may not find a solution to them and probably never an escape from them. In spite of our best intentions, we are only human and so will sometimes fail to be as ethical as we should be; being human, we will ourselves often be confused, just like our students, about the just and ethical course to take. Even with our best efforts, we will inadvertently ignore or hurt a student. And who is going to be so selfless as always to surrender personal interests to those of others?

Nevertheless, the ethics of teaching gains a certain clarity by virtue of its unwavering focus on students' welfare. Rather than appearing as sanctimony, teachers' ethical responsibilities ought to be broadening, bracing, and enhancing. They ought to indicate not righteousness but firmness of heart. By holding to the long view of what is in their students' best interests—their learning, their moral development, the creation in them of an aspiration always to try to surpass what they have previously known and achieved—teachers see to it that all teaching justifies itself.

☙☙☙

MOST OF us have benefited from the teaching of people who are not by occupation teachers. Such people seem to fall into their teaching role without thinking about it, all the while understanding, without being told, that their teaching will and should be judged against the same standards as those of professional teachers—whether their instruction is sound, whether it benefits those who learn from them, whether it can be taken in like sugar rather than medicine, whether it is just and ethical. One of these amateur teachers was Emily Patterson, "Aunt Em" to her family.

An accountant by trade ("I prefer to manipulate numbers, not people"), an aunt by nature, Aunt Em had never married, but she had four siblings who had. And by them she had acquired ten nieces and nephews. This could have had little or no effect on her life, but she was the kind of person who took her family responsibilities seriously, who was naturally delighted to be among young people, and who was unselfish to a degree that astonished others. She gave up weekends to care for her nieces and nephews when she might have been traveling with friends. She moved into her brothers' and sisters' houses to look after the children when their parents were away. Her chief satisfactions in life derived from putting the welfare of each before her own and devoting most of her leisure to assisting the children's growth from childhood into adulthood. Not surprisingly, Emily became in the children's lives a kind of third parent, an auxiliary mother.

But while learning the tastes, interests, and enthusiasms of each of them and being their favorite gift-giver, she also knew that she had to honor the boundary between their parents and herself. She never took advantage of the children's credulity by trying to transfer their affection for their parents into her account. She understood that all parents were the resented rule-setters, those who established boundaries with stiff insistence, and she knew that the affection the children felt for them was hard to earn. So she never interfered in that relationship but instead tried to develop her own with them, always careful to maintain limits on her own behavior. The result was that, captivated by the ten youngsters, she gained the devotion and respect of all of them in return.

Emily was one of those people to whom teaching comes naturally, whatever they do. We usually think of teachers as professionally trained people hired and paid to teach in schools and colleges. Most of us experience at least twelve years of our lives being taught by them, and we never forget them, both the good ones and the bad, because, for better or worse, they shaped much of our lives. Professional teachers play so prominent a role in our formative experiences that it takes some effort to recognize that teaching happens all the time throughout life at the hands of people we do not think of as teachers at all and who may not think of themselves as teachers, either. Among them, our parents and other family members are our teachers in early years. But others can be our teachers, too, when as adults we encounter them as doctors, nurses, ministers, rabbis, priests, counselors, office managers, policemen, lawyers, colleagues, and supervisors of all kinds. They can be found everywhere. They are experienced people. For some of them, teaching is simply part of who they are; for others, trying to pass on their knowledge and wisdom, usually to a younger generation, seems an easy responsibility, so they accept it with pleasure. Some of these teachers are paid for their efforts (with parents occasionally thinking that they, too, are due a stipend); but often they teach gratis and out of the goodness of their hearts.

So it was for Aunt Em. For example, there was Billy, aged eight and crazy about large mammals, lions in particular. Aunt Em helped him find Africa in an atlas, downloaded films about lions' natural habitat and behavior, and took him to the zoo, where he confronted his first big carnivore. Billy was thrilled and told his mother about the animals as she put him to bed that night. "But you know, Mom," he suddenly exclaimed, "Aunt Em is really weird." Puzzled, she asked him, "Why do you say that?" "She likes snakes," Billy responded with disgust. Years later, after Billy had become William and a veterinarian, Aunt Em was there to see him throw his cap in the air and wave his diploma. "What a pity!" she muttered to herself. "He would have made a great herpetologist." William never had learned her true views. She had mentioned her fascination with snakes but never tried to steer him away from his true interest.

Snakes were not Aunt Em's only enthusiasm; in fact, it was hard to find anything that failed to arouse her curiosity and interest. Music was another of her passions, and she tried to take all of it in—from High Baroque to rock 'n' roll, even hip hop. This humble woman's instrument was the flute ("If proud Alcibiades scorned it," she was once heard to say, "then it's just the thing for me"), so it failed to surprise anyone that two of her nieces adopted the same instrument and played well enough to earn chairs in their school and college orchestras. Aunt Em got to share in their pleasure because they always brought home for additional practice, as well as for her fun, their solo passages. Emily always said it was better to be able to play the music than to hear even a great orchestra bring it alive. "Walking a mile in somebody else's shoes" she called it, an essential, empathic skill for everyone to have, even when sitting down.

Always treading lightly and ceding to her brothers and sisters their own children's disciplining, she never in return surrendered her own views of what was right and wrong. She also knew that what the best and most well-intentioned parent or anyone else might try to teach a child could come across as harsh nagging and turn counterproductive. She might occasionally be found trying to slip in a lesson without intruding, but like everyone else, even when trying not to, she could also occasionally step over the line. At one of her family's gatherings, Emily was saddened, as she had been before, by the absence of the children's grandparents. Two had died, and the two others lived at a distance. The result was that the children had no close association with the elderly and seemed to find the older people they met so strange as to have been members of a different species.

Shortly after this particular family gathering, Emily was troubled by the derisive comments her nephews were making about old people they passed in the street. They "walked funny" and "always scowled." Dismayed by what she overheard the children saying, she lost her temper and scolded them. Recovering her calm, Aunt Em apologized for her outburst and explained why their lack of consideration for others deserved rebuke. They would be old themselves one day, she pointed out to them, and would look then for courtesy and help from others. Teaching the children, she told herself, could be her role, but she worried that stepping into their parents' shoes was harder to justify. How could she improve on that lesson?

A few years before, she had volunteered at the local senior center to drive old people to their medical appointments and assist them with their shopping needs. So she began to slip tales of the lives of these people into conversations with her nieces and nephews. Then she started taking the youngsters with her on her volunteer rounds and getting them to help her elderly friends with climbing steps and carrying their groceries. She said nothing about her intentions as the schoolchildren heard her friends reminisce about such ancient events as the Depression and World War Two and life—could it ever have really been that way?—before there was television, air conditioning, and texting. Emily was heard to joke about needing a larger car to accommodate all the willing volunteers who clamored for seats. There were no more nasty remarks about the elderly.

The years went by, and soon her nieces and nephews began producing the next generation of family members for Emily's attention. After a vigorous and sturdy old age, and after being helped up steps and with her marketing—"walking in others' shoes"—she died at the age of ninety-three. William gave the eulogy and said of her, "She was the best teacher I ever had." At the reception afterward, one of his relatives tried to contradict him. "Aunt Emily was never a teacher," she declared. William smiled and said, very firmly, "Oh yes, she was."

⪆ Order

MANY OF THE WORLD'S COMMANDING MYTHS explain the origins of human culture by describing the creation of the world as the imposition of order on chaos. The credibility and appeal of the myths have depended in part on our innate sense that harmony must replace discord, that chance must give place to certainty, and that direction must substitute for indirection if human society is to exist. It is also generally understood that incentives and sometimes even coercion are necessary for the creation of order because disorder always resists being rearranged into order. Thus the shaping and maintenance of structure, within the self as well as within society, is always to some extent a painful process, exacting costs even while bestowing benefits. Yet we all seem to agree that some kind of order is needed if any measure of improvement in the conditions of human existence is to occur.

It is hardly surprising, therefore, that teaching reflects what society itself demands; it necessitates that disorder—of students and teachers alike, of mind, behavior, and environment—yield to its opposite. Effective teaching requires that, failing their own self-imposed order, students experience the imposition of some outer order so that inner order may develop. This means in practice, for instance, that the goals of classes and courses be clearly set, that they be explained and justified, that the manner of achieving them be clear, that the presentation of materials conducive to reaching them be appropriate, and that all activities be directed somehow to their attainment. It means, too, that students take up their own obligation to maintain the conditions under which learning occurs: quiet in their classrooms, respect for and courtesy toward others, civility of language and behavior, and the like. Above all, it implies structured industry—study and activity that are oriented toward a goal and pursued with perseverance and method. That is, good teaching requires that teachers and students subject themselves to external and internal control so that learning can take place.

Discipline is part of order. The notion of "discipline," which has so many alarming connotations for so many people, does not deserve its negative reputation, for it means much more than punishment or rules. In teaching, as in so many other things, discipline connotes the kind of training that molds and perfects knowledge and character. It also connotes the very qualities of orderliness, self-control, and good conduct that are essential to learning. Thus, discipline is a positive force, not a mere limitation on behavior.

Discipline must be an attribute of teachers as well as of students. Much classroom discipline has to do with a teacher's acceptance of the obligation to be disciplined in behavior—that is, to be orderly, clear, accurate, and authentic in expression and purpose so as to be able to teach well and to serve the students' good.

What kindles objections, what so often summons up grim images of oppression, of tyrants, martinets, and dictators—of all the villains of history as well as the stock characters of melodrama who oppose liberty and freedom—is the notion of teachers' bringing discipline to their students. Limits on students' freedom of thought, behavior, or expression, we hear it said, threaten their welfare and their natural selves. Yet teachers who exercise discipline prudently never neglect the good of their students, nor are they guilty of limiting their students' freedom. On the contrary: the teachers are serving that freedom by creating in their students the capacities to manage—by knowledgeable thought, clear expression, considered behavior —the natural confusions of human life.

Discipline is therefore the means teachers must use to impose necessary organization on the potential chaos of all classrooms, and they must do so to create an atmosphere favorable to learning. Discipline takes many forms: schedules, rules of conduct, exemplary behavior, and clear expectations, as well as an equitable system of rewards and penalties. A system of positive and negative incentives, if it is to be fair and effective and if it is to maintain the right balance between excessive rigor and debilitating laxity, gives students a sense of the bounds within which they may act freely in the interests of learning.

Such discipline, necessary to the creation of order, implies the possibility of punishment. Physical chastisement is not acceptable. It is not among most teachers' options, nor is there any need for its restoration; we have come to have confidence that we may spare the rod without spoiling the child. The cruelty of a teacher like Wackford Squeers in Dickens's *Nicholas Nickleby* is probably even more repugnant to us than it was to the novel's original readers. Squeers is an ignorant, violent, greedy man, totally unfit to be a teacher, a person from whose company society should protect its young. Nevertheless, banishing from the classroom the kind of corporal punishment he inflicted has not—and probably never will—rid teaching of unjustifiable harshness and damaging thoughtlessness. The cruelest weapons today's teachers possess are the tongue and the sneer; what teachers say or fail to say, and the way they offer praise or blame, can determine the degree to which order prevails in their classrooms.

What teachers say, however, whether they mean to approve or to reprimand, is not the only means of achieving good order. Example speaks as loud as words. A teacher who is industrious and punctual can justifiably expect those virtues of students. Teachers who use their own time to satisfy students' curiosity, who return assignments edited with helpful comments and suggestions soon after they have been submitted, who allow no time to be wasted in or out of their classrooms—these are the teachers who experience the least difficulty in persuading their students to accept and practice the organization required for learning.

While the ways to create order are many and differ with each level of student, there are some common aspects of order that characterize all good teaching.

Order requires the exertion of authority. Authority is the principal means by which order and discipline are created and maintained in the classroom. Feckless teachers or those who think of themselves as students' equals are not likely to be able to establish the ordered environment and dependable conditions in which serious learning can take place. Students must be able to depend upon their teachers to maintain quiet in their classrooms, to proceed in a comprehensible fashion from one lesson to the next, to make learning the central activity of their classes, and to create an atmosphere of equitable and ethical behavior. Without the exemplification of order in teachers' very bearing—an order that manifests itself in attitude as well as idea, in spirit as well as in work—learning is difficult to come by, and its value is discounted.

A teacher's first encounter with a new group of students thus bears much importance in this respect. A teacher who is all business and no nonsense at the initial meeting of a class risks a certain stiffness in the greater interest of being able to relax once the ground rules for work have been established. Too much familiarity and easiness at the outset are likely to make for greater difficulty later on, when the need for order and authority requires some distance and rigor.

Order arises from a teacher's leadership. Teachers, not students, must establish the organization and atmosphere of their classrooms. A secret of instruction lies in a teacher's ability to get their students to follow where they seek deliberately to lead. For while closely linked to authority, leadership embodies intent and direction. Teachers must make clear their purposes in teaching each lesson and must relate it to their students' own welfare in ways that the students themselves can understand. In doing so, teachers both establish the orderly and comprehensible external structure in which teaching can take place and help create the internal mental order without which students cannot learn. Once teachers are clear in the goals they have in mind and the intellectual and moral compass by which they steer toward them, students are more likely to adapt to the teachers' standards and, no matter how rigorous the demands of learning may be, rise to their challenge.

Most teachers know where they are going but often forget that they must communicate their direction and goals before starting to move toward them. "Follow me!" may be a stirring command, but students are likely to want to know where they are going and why they should want to go there. Good teachers anticipate and answer such questions before they are asked.

Order requires teaching to have direction and momentum. Which of us does not remember a history teacher who announced at the beginning of the year that the course would span the nation's history up to the present day but then, in dithering over provisions of this and that act, telling tales about this and that prominent figure, and pausing to discuss topics unrelated to the course, never got beyond 1932? Or a biology instructor who never carried the class beyond worms, when mammals were still to be studied? Such teachers fail for lack of orientation and impetus toward their own established goals; they let down their students, many of whom have internalized some expectations about the course's contents; and they endanger students' welfare by denying them further, promised knowledge. They know how to cover materials but not how to create from those materials a coherent whole; they know how to raise issues but not how to make their presentation aesthetically pleasing and intellectually satisfying for having been concluded, not just terminated by the calendar. Courses, like many things in life, are hard to end; but far more satisfying is a genuine conclusion than an abrupt cessation, and a goal achieved is better by far than one abandoned.

Order implies tranquility in the classroom. There are, of course, always appropriate occasions for creative disorder and noise—when children are learning through games, in the laughter of a class, during staged experiments and demonstrations. Where there is error, a teacher can adjust and establish truth; but confusion is no basis for constructive work of any sort. Learning is not likely to take place when a classroom is always noisy or continually disorderly for want of a teacher's authority. Learning has no chance in a climate in which knowledge and its pursuit are not taken seriously. A classroom's calm and quiet environment allows students to fix their attention on the teacher, whose instruction can then be heard and understood.

Yet to create this classroom tranquillity, teachers must themselves try to be calm. A teacher's practiced, even-tempered bearing may not mute all the chaos toward which many groups of students naturally incline, but serenity at the front of the classroom is always preferable to a raised voice or the aspect of confusion. This does not mean that an occasional teacherly outburst or a stern rebuke ought never to be employed to discipline unruly or impertinent students. But such sharp punctuations should be rare and exceptional. Then, of course, they are likely to have their maximum effect—and calm may settle in once again.

Order involves discipline. Yet discipline necessitates neither reproof nor punishment. What it does require is clarity of expectation, appropriate correction, justifiable penalty for infraction, and forgiveness. Consistency, dependability, and fairness equal good discipline. Reprimands need be no more than calm, simple statements of faults, coupled with expressions of disapproval and disappointment on the teacher's part. They should always be followed by something hopeful and positive, something to indicate that students' errors should not be repeated and something to suggest ways of avoiding them in the future. Students should be left with the sense that the matter has been addressed and dismissed as past experience and that the teacher bears no grudge and still has an open mind about the student who has been found momentarily wanting.

Good teachers always try to turn experiences that may discourage their students into encouraging ones. The teacher's object, after all, is to get students to do better, not to demonstrate superior understanding or to provide exemplary punishment. A student who, upon being corrected, concludes that the teacher "thinks I'm stupid" or "expects too much of me" is likely to be a student lost to learning.

Order should be accepted as good. The structure established by good teachers makes learning possible. Therefore that structure must be good if it facilitates a good result. Yet many students see the discipline necessary to that structure as an enemy, as something externally imposed, as something to be resisted if they can get away with it. A good teacher will be aware of this attitude, will argue against it, and will provide incentives for making order pleasing and discipline acceptable. All games are organized by rules, and the young are usually quick to accept such rules on the playground and in the gymnasium. But they are often reluctant to acknowledge the importance of rules and order in the classroom. Good teachers work hard to see that they do.

The language of discipline, of course, has its drawbacks. We speak of the enforcement of discipline, and its metaphors are often those of curbs and whips. But good teachers know that effective discipline is not external at all. The discipline that matters, that outlives all other kinds, is inner, self-imposed, and self-accepted order. Effective teachers must therefore encourage, whenever and wherever they can, the growth of inner order by demonstrating its advantages in the environment of their classrooms and by furnishing living examples of its benefits in their own behavior.

Order necessitates that teachers set good examples. The virtues expected of students must first be evident in teachers: industry, patience, punctuality, honesty, clarity, perseverance, seriousness, dependability, and consideration. Habits of self-discipline in a teacher provide models for their students and justify teachers' high expectations of those they teach. While intelligence may be innate, organization requires long practice and assiduous discipline. In this context, teachers must be ready to reveal appropriate dimensions of their personal habits and professional lives out of school in order to establish models of behavior for their students. If teachers keep journals to improve their writing skills or read some Spanish prose or poetry every day to maintain their language competence, they should not hesitate to mention such practice to their students when it seems natural to bring it up—not to impress their students with their erudition or industry, but to stimulate the students' curiosity and imitation.

Order requires the maintenance of standards. These standards should be set by teachers so that they are always a little beyond the capacities of their students. Robert Browning summed it up by declaring that our reach should exceed our grasp, "or what's a heaven for?" A test on which anyone gets 100 percent is not fully measuring the achievement of that student. Thus students should always be striving to outdo themselves but not to the point of being discouraged into feeling that there is no point in trying. "Demanding but fair" is a good description of an effective teacher, but "too demanding" is a condemnation in itself. Students are learning satisfactorily when they are regularly reaching for the almost-attainable.

Standards range from minor ones (such as the appropriate form for written assignments) to major ones (such as how much a student must know about the reproductive systems of various kinds of animals in order to meet the requirements of a biology course). No matter what their level of importance, expecting strict adherence to all standards—the reasons for all of which should be openly explained—is a mark of all good teaching. Form may be of slighter consequence than substance, but to yield in small matters makes it harder to maintain standards when they really count.

In the end, the maintenance of order in teaching creates respect for knowledge and for those who are learning. Both are prerequisites for the act of teaching itself. Reciprocally, respect for learning creates the condition for order. Disorder is the enemy of teaching because it is foreign to knowledge. The world may not be orderly or coherent, but knowledge of the world, even of its very incoherence, must be orderly—as must be its pursuit. Teachers who can order their words, their presentations, and their goals are more likely than those who cannot to teach their students well and thus to recruit them to a lifelong effort to learn.

⇜ ⇜ ⇜

FOR MORE THAN TWENTY YEARS students had been stunned by their first meeting with Peggy Minton. Other teachers whose instruction they had enjoyed or endured in the previous eight grades had shown varying degrees of organization and discipline in their styles of teaching, but these teachers all seemed vague, uncoordinated, and dilatory compared with Ms. Minton, who taught first-year Latin with a zestful diligence that many regarded as fanatical.

Ninth-graders come in all shapes and sizes, but most of hers were taller than Peggy Minton, who measured little more than five feet. But what she lacked in height she made up for in energy by establishing control in the first moments of meeting every new group of students.

In the early fall, when she entered the classroom for the first time, she would put her books and papers on her desk and stand facing her students and awaiting their complete silence. She would remain quite still, her trim figure poised like a bird about to take flight, her eyes darting about the room as though deciding where she might land. When the silence was absolute and the waiting had become an embarrassment for the more sensitive, she would speak.

"Good morning." There would be an inarticulate murmur, accompanied by some scraping of the feet, nervous giggling, some coughing. When the silence resumed, Ms. Minton would say rather sharply, "That was not an appropriate response. I expect you to wish me good morning clearly and in unison. I have greeted you civilly, and I expect no less in return. Good morning."

This time the students would usually manage to coordinate a coherent "Good morning," and Ms. Minton would continue. "That's better. It tells me that I have your complete attention, and that we can get to work immediately. But there's a boy"— there would always be one—"in the back row who has something to say. Yes, you—I'm sorry I don't know your names yet—you have a question or comment?"

"No, Ms. Minton."

"Then you're wasting our time by making comments to your neighbor. What's your name?"

"Julian Johnson."

"Thank you, Julian. Now tell me what you have learned so far."

The boy would frown as if thought was a strain and then inevitably say something like, "You start every class by saying 'Good morning.'"

"Correct—and . . . ?"

Another pause for thought, and then, as if by sudden inspiration, "You want us to say 'Good morning' back to you."

"And why do I do that?"

"Because it means you have our complete attention and we're ready to start work."

"And one more thing?"

"We can't talk to each other during class."

"Good! Let's proceed."

The class would fall apart in all directions struggling with three-ring binders, pencil boxes, and book bags. "This is taking much too long," Ms. Minton would declare, still waiting for the last students to find their pens and pencils. "So here's a new rule: when you say 'Good morning' to me, you will have paper ready in front of you and a pen or pencil in your hand. Ready to work means ready to write! Or, as we say in this class, *Paratus laborare, paratus scribere*."

As she spoke these words, she would write her last words on the blackboard in both English and Latin, turn around and say briskly, "Write it down!" The class would copy the words. Every face in the room would look up for her next instruction.

As Ms. Minton began, so she continued. By the end of fifty minutes, she had outlined the purposes of her course in Latin for the entire year, memorized the names of each of her thirty students, had direct conversation with at least twenty of them, introduced them to the textbook, given them their first assignment, and wasted not one second of her time or theirs.

Every student in the class formed the same first impression: that she knew exactly what she was doing, that she was determined to do what she set out to do, and that it would be best to avoid crossing her or failing to come up to her expectations. Even the brightest of them found their new teacher sharper, better informed, and more thoroughly organized than they were; they recognized in her a spirit of adventure and of challenge; and they were left a little breathless at the end of the hour.

First impressions are one thing, but staying the course was another of Peggy Minton's virtues. She maintained her brisk style and hustling encouragement of students consistently throughout the year. Not only that, her standards were rigorous and high. Because of that, most of her students aspired to achieve them, and those who could not do so received too much reinforcement from her for their efforts to feel that they had failed. In addition, she fully explained her grading aims and methods in general terms to the class at large and in frequent conferences with students and sometimes with their parents. As a result of what others saw as her fairness and just expectations, her students usually rose beyond their own conception of their potential; the consensus among them, even among the most grudging, was that they had never worked so hard for any other teacher.

First-year Latin is mostly a matter of memorization. The many inflections of the parts of speech, their significance in sentences, and the scrupulous accuracy with which these distinctions must be identified, interpreted, and translated—all these tasks were simplified for her students by Ms. Minton's careful and patient explanations. Her students prided themselves on being able to distinguish between *scribit, scribet,* and *scribat;* and their understanding of the forms of English grammar marched right along with their acquisition of this strange, foreign, and long-"dead" language. Learn the rules, memorize the exceptions, and apply your knowledge to the business of translation,

Ms. Minton would remind her students continually. She had little need to enforce discipline in her classes. Her students sensed that any breach of good order would prompt a sharp reaction in a teacher who insisted that every action on their part be deliberate and appropriate. They knew how she reacted when the most trifling matters went wrong; they did not like to imagine what her reaction would be to any major breakdown of good order in her classroom. Nor would she waste her time with the equivocations of the mischievous and the indolent. She gave them such short shrift that they enjoyed only the pity of their peers—a far cry from the popularity and admiration that had prompted their attempts at disruption in some other classrooms.

At the end of the year, most of her students came to the same conclusion about Ms. Minton's teaching: that she was clear, demanding, and fair, and that, if you paid attention, you always knew exactly what you had to do to succeed. The clarity of structure in her classroom enabled all of them, even the most typically lazy or uncaring, to learn. Even though they wondered if she was not something of an oddball to have such an enthusiastic interest in such a quantity of detail, the lessons of methodical organization, discipline, and industry stayed with them long after they had forgotten the curious inflections of Latin verbs.

✑ Imagination

BEHIND ALL GOOD TEACHING, though rarely acknowledged, lies teachers' ambition for all students they have ever taught—that their students be more knowledgeable, more open to life, more understanding of the world than when they first entered the teachers' classrooms. Good teachers thus have the ability somehow to imagine themselves in their students' places and then to help those students imagine themselves in other times, locations, and circumstances not immediately present to their senses and, for the most part, never previously experienced. Teachers—whether teaching physics, literature, or arithmetic—thus lose a bit of themselves in their students while helping them lose themselves in their subjects. This is what William James had in mind in his valuable *Talks to Teachers*. "In teaching, you must simply work your pupil into such a state of interest in what you are going to teach him," he wrote in the old-fashioned masculine way, "that every other subject of attention is banished from his mind; then reveal it to him so impressively that he will remember the occasion to his dying day; and finally fill him with devouring curiosity to know what the next steps in connection with the subject are."

The "state of interest" to which James referred can exist only if students' minds are prepared to be interested. Without prepared minds, students are not likely to learn. Yet how do teachers prepare their students' minds? First they learn the ways to interest them—by imagining how to capture their attention, get them to work hard and gain satisfaction from doing so, and make knowledge relevant to their lives. The key to that preparation will differ from student to student. So good teachers try to contrive ways of using their students' varied interests to lead them to learn on their own.

This need to help others transcend their own lives is required by the very challenge of transmitting knowledge; teachers must prepare their students' minds to acquire knowledge by imagining what possessing it might mean for them. The urge to do so is prompted by an empathetic regard for their situations, for they are mostly young, dependent, comparatively ignorant, and inexperienced. They need help, and teachers must figure out how to help them.

In this, imagination has to be assisted by memory. Teachers must summon recollections of their own struggles to learn, must recall their own frustrations and failures to grasp their teachers' lessons when they were at their students' own stage of learning. Imagination must also be complemented by compassion, by a teacher's understanding of the energies students expend and the risks to their accustomed ways of thinking they assume in gaining any knowledge. It is thus imagination, above all other elements of teaching, that requires teachers to see themselves again at another, earlier stage of life with lesser, because comparatively less formed, intellectual powers—a stage now occupied by their students. The process is much the same as in films and plays, when the director anticipates the impressions of audiences and guides the actors accordingly. Good teachers accomplish the same ends by analogous means;

they project themselves into the minds of their students to estimate their capacity for learning, to anticipate their reactions to instruction, and to envision their use of knowledge.

In some respects, there is no such thing as "unimaginative teaching." The term is an oxymoron; the simple act of teaching always involves a stretching of the mind into a fresh state of awareness. But there are unimaginative teachers; they are the ones who make no effort to understand or to enter into their students' minds and spirits or to engage fully the subjects they teach. Yet all teachers, except for the most obtuse and cynical, believe that their teaching will be effective, that their students will learn, and that the goals they set are within their students' reach. That belief is based on the clarity with which teachers can envisage their students' future lives and can articulate a vision of what is possible for their students, who do not yet know what they are capable of achieving.

Imagination is also the quality that allows teachers to tackle subject matter in novel and attractive ways. Playing with knowledge, finding fresh and distinctive approaches to putting facts and arguments together, requires teachers to respond to the interests and situations of their students. Even the most matter-of-fact material, like multiplication tables, gains appeal through relevant examples and illustrated use. Imagination also usually requires casting loose from the contents of textbooks and prescribed curricular plans. Imaginative teachers illuminate and clarify material before their students encounter it in their textbooks; in that way, students are more prepared and open to the lessons the textbooks have to teach. Imaginative teachers do much more than merely echo those dry if essential books; after all, they know more than the books' authors of the needs and receptivity to knowledge of their particular students.

Imaginative teachers are also sufficiently aware of their students and their place in the world to be able to choose lessons and examples that will prompt their students' more conscious recognition of dimensions of their own lives in the subject matter at hand. This need not—should not—be an intrusion on the privacy of students but a tool that teachers can make good use of in assisting their students to attain new learning and new levels of comprehension.

Being infinite in its range and variety, how can imagination serve teaching?

Imagination in teaching begins with confidence that knowledge is transferable. Teachers cannot teach without hope, without the conviction that their efforts to bring what they know to the attention of their students and to introduce them to the possibility of a similar level of understanding will be effective. Teachers must believe that there will always be some chink or aperture, no matter how well hidden and obscure, which they can widen into an avenue for discourse between one mind and another; they must believe in the ability of others to gain knowledge, and then they must visualize how they can best get them to receive it. Teachers of first-year Spanish know that all students in their classes have the capacity to speak Spanish more fluently than they think they can; but which of the students believes this to be possible? The cry from them is always, "This is too hard! We can't understand it! We'll never learn it!" The teacher's response must always be, "I know. That's the way it was for me, too. At first, it seemed impossible. But look, it's not so hard. Even I learned it! Let me explain. Of course you can understand. You'll be able to learn this. Let me show you how."

Imaginative teachers find their own ways to enhance learning. Finding those ways is part of the true art of teaching because the ways of helping others to learn are infinitely varied. Each student, each classroom, each subject, and each occasion challenges each teacher to reconsider the best means of introducing knowledge to others. In reevaluating each new situation, a teacher must always be aware of changes, however slight, in each student; a teacher's response to new circumstances must be fresh. Thus imagination is among the most demanding components of teaching, for the success of teaching depends largely on a teacher's rigorous and continual evaluation and reevaluation of students' moods, maturity, aptitude, attitude, and character. To know students well, to understand how their minds work, to recognize their limitations and deficiencies—these are all necessary for excellent teaching, and they are all achieved by the exercise of the imagination.

Though teachers' own lives may be enriched by their work, it is the lives of their students that ought to be transformed by knowledge; to achieve this, teachers must project themselves into those other minds. In this way, imaginative teachers understand students well enough to anticipate and remove their difficulties and confusion in confronting any new body of material even before their students identify those difficulties. Yet the virtues of careful planning must be balanced by spontaneity, by a teacher's comfort in the unplanned and unrehearsed. It requires confidence for teachers to launch themselves into uncharted flights of experiment and play, for freshness and charm can result in bumpy landings. But as long as such voyages are closely linked to the subject their students are studying, the excitement and enthusiasm they generate make the risks involved worth taking.

Imagination means visualizing students' futures. Teaching is never an act unto itself; it always invites students to enter into a world of infinite possibilities of thought and vision. And yet the purpose of teaching is to enrich students' minds and spirits so that they can lead full lives through their understanding of life itself. How they will do so, and how well, can never be known to a teacher in advance. But it is in a teacher's power—indeed it is a teacher's responsibility—to envision what knowledge can mean to the students in any particular class; no less important is envisioning what that knowledge might mean later and helping students to understand that, too. This often means that teachers must relate to their students how particular knowledge has affected their own lives, or help them to see how mastery of particularly difficult material—say, mathematical equations for those anticipating business careers, or the histories of other nations for those who wish to become diplomats—might advance their prospects to achieve what they seek. Knowledge can then be seen to open not just students' minds but possibilities in their lives; teaching then becomes a key into others' futures, and it helps get them there.

Imagination anticipates the needs and reactions of students. "Imagination," wrote Shakespeare in *A Midsummer Night's*

Dream, "bodies forth the forms of things unknown." And as we all know, the unknown stimulates fears as easily as it generates hope. Teachers must present what students do not yet know in attractive and positive forms; and by understanding their students' uncertainty when facing strange obstacles, they will be assisted in this task. They must convince students that they can master new subject matter, play with new knowledge, and create their own understanding of the world. Such confidence, which is founded on a teacher's own experience and knowledge, is infectious when imagination works to make it so. If students have confidence in their teachers, they will also have confidence in their ability to learn and to succeed.

Imagination enhances and facilitates the presentation of subject matter. Embarking on a new topic in the classroom is always a difficult and delicate matter. Textbooks do not usually offer teachers much help with the preparation of their students for the shock of the new. In an English grammar textbook, a chapter on participles, for example, will often offer a definition, identify the forms of participles, list examples, and provide some rules for the use of verbal adjectives in sentences, and it may end with a warning against unattached or "dangling" participles. Yet merely escorting students through the chapter will have little effect on their understanding. Imaginative teachers will go further by considering the role of participles in describing the lives of their students. They may make a list of pertinent phrases—watching television, eating lunch, driving cars, reading books—and then point out the difference between verbal nouns, or gerunds, and verbal adjectives, or participles. "A writing desk," they will insist, "is a desk designed for writing, while a writing student is not a surface." In other words, good teachers will make the strange familiar and the unintelligible obvious by imagining their students' difficulties in advance.

Imagination in teaching means being successfully creative. Imaginative teachers believe that teaching, as an art, involves fashioning qualities in their students that were not present before. Effective teachers every day manage to transform uncertainty into knowledge—an achievement that approaches the alchemy of making something from nothing. And while every such success is unique, each has predictable attributes. Each usually requires departure from routine, or even an inversion of customary practice, to achieve its effects. It often involves taking risks. It may take the form of announcing at the first meeting of a class that everyone starts with the grade of F and must work to deserve better, or its opposite—that everyone starts with an A and must work to keep the grade there. And if a teacher's creative attempt fails one day, the next day imagination must work to find a more effective route to pedagogical success. For what teachers are seeking to do is to rivet their students' attention on study, to encourage aspiration, and to inspire learning.

Imagination introduces surprise and excitement into teaching. While some predictability is essential to teaching and learning, especially in the early grades, students regard imagination, which to them connotes the unpredictable, the fantastic, the mysterious, and the make-believe, as their particular province. And should they not? The games that begin with "Let's pretend . . ." and the flights of fancy launched with "Let's suppose . . ." are so common among children that the young are often surprised and delighted to discover imagination in their teachers. Those teachers are the ones who can bring theory to life; who put on costumes, makeup, or masks to impersonate historical characters; or who devise field trips that turn regional resources into sites of learning. Imagination that is yoked to learning and experience can carry students far beyond the reach of their own imaginative powers. Imagination kindles imagination.

Teaching is always an act of faith. It requires that teachers perform unceasing imaginative leaps to conceive what may be possible for others to learn and to do, to think and to feel. Teachers must venture into the expansive realm of possibilities; they must continually suspend any fear that something may not be within reach of their students. It is this quality of suspending fear that makes great teaching evangelical and sometimes irresistible. Its power arises from a teacher's sustaining faith in the capacity of knowledge and understanding to enrich life, even when faced with the customary intractability of the human mind to enlarge itself. In this urge to conceive correctly what others may know and what they may accomplish with knowledge lie the sources of effective teaching and the resources with which teachers continually replenish themselves.

Imagination in teaching thus has more to do with potential than with realization. It allows a teacher to take each achievement of instruction as an invitation to envisage the outcome of the next challenge and the ones after that, to picture the realization of that which has not yet been realized. Like so many other dimensions of teaching, imagination is a quality of vision and spirit; it must be summoned from within.

༄ ༄ ༄

A FERTILE IMAGINATION was Matthew Millstein's most notable attribute as a teacher. He approached the improvement of the writing skills of college freshmen with all the zest and enthusiasm of a seven-year-old attacking an ice cream sundae at a birthday party. Freshman comp does not generally gladden the hearts of those called to teach it (which is the reason, as someone once remarked, why God created graduate students); it has all the deadening qualities of the proverbial millstone (as our eponymous professor was well aware), and most of us prefer other forms of neckwear. But Professor Millstein loved his trade and brought a freshness and vitality to all his classes that aroused the envy—although, unfortunately, not the emulation—of his colleagues.

It is well known that those most in need of help with their writing are those who most hate writing courses. They are also the ones for whom required writing courses are particularly designed. The challenge offered to teachers of mandatory writing courses may therefore be unmatched anywhere else in the curriculum. Yet before his captive and resentful audiences, Matthew Millstein took up his challenge gladly and turned most of his ugly, illiterate frogs into articulate and handsome princes and princesses by semester's end.

The magic was in the Millsteinian imagination. As Dr. Millstein told his students when he first met with them, his vision of their future was of all of them as prolific and published authors.

He told them about Michelangelo's facing a block of marble and chipping away the extraneous matter to discover the statue within. Like Michelangelo, he saw his task as removing whatever obstacles lay between his students and the improvement of their writing. "To find out what those obstacles are," he would declare, "I will need a sample from each of you. Nothing brief, mind you! Something multipaged and detailed, encompassing the kind of tricky subject matter you will be expected to write about in your other courses at this institution, whatever the major of your choice. And please fill your samples with as many errors, neologisms, spelling mistakes, syntactical monstrosities, and solecisms as possible. Give me your writing, like marble hacked from the quarry, and let me be the sculptor who uncovers the beauty beneath the surface."

Professor Millstein's conviction that all his students were destined to become accomplished writers meant that he was genuinely interested in what they wrote, no matter how inept, awkward, and ill-phrased their early efforts might be. His comments and criticisms were always encouraging, and he came close to entering into a continuing correspondence with each of them, even though his classes averaged some thirty-five students apiece. The self-assumed workload was of course backbreaking. He wrote many responses to his students' work by hand, but most of the time he preferred to use e-mail and encouraged his students to respond by the same means. These individual exchanges might occur two or three times a week.

Professor Millstein's classroom presentations of difficult subjects were always illuminated by his novel approaches—many of which he conceived and practiced by himself before using.

In considering complex sentences, for instance, he would explain indirect speech and questions and clarify relative clauses. When he had covered these constructions, he would take up the other nine types of subordinate clause, those usually described as adverbial. In case students had difficulty remembering these, he had a little mnemonic verse ready for them:

Come, Cuthbert, Cause Paul Pleasure;
Tread Round a Roguish Measure!

This nonsensical couplet gave his students the initial letters of the nine types of adverbial subordinate clause: conditional, concessive, comparative, purpose, place, time, result, reason, and manner. He taught about them, not because they were essential for everyone to know, but to illustrate the wonderful complexity of his beloved language. Yet his charges rarely forgot them—even the great majority who did not become writers.

As well as writing for each other, the students in his classes were expected to write for publication, too. He encouraged them to send letters and other pieces to the student newspaper, and there were usually three or four each semester who had letters published in the local press. For texts in class, Professor Millstein often used newspapers and magazines to prompt his students to write for the public, and he set a model for them by showing them his own letters and articles when they appeared in various newspapers and magazines.

While Dr. Millstein's classes were orderly and his intentions clear, his instructional methods were frequently novel, and excitement was always in the air. Students never knew precisely what to expect; Professor Millstein would use any means to clarify a point of grammar or elucidate a problem of style. Wearing funny hats, singing and dancing, making up games for his students to play, attempting conjuring tricks, distributing candy as a reward for participation in class discussion—nothing seemed too much trouble or too ridiculous if it helped his students improve their writing skills. Because he was consistently serious in his purposes, none of these gimmicks detracted from his authority as a teacher. In fact, he was held throughout the campus in great respect because these methods indicated to others that he was putting additional time and effort into his teaching.

Quick to anticipate students' reactions, Professor Millstein also had a reputation as something of a mind reader; he seemed able to predict questions, forestall complaints, and prevent difficulties almost before they had arisen. He attributed this talent to the fact that he had a strong recollection of his own years as a student; he was always ready to relate his own confusion and ineptitude in those far-off days for the instruction of his classes.

"In high school," he would tell them, "my writing was so awful that when I asked my English teacher what I should write on, she told me privately that she thought one side of an index card would be quite sufficient.

"Another time I asked my teacher what I could do to improve my writing. He sat there thinking for such a long time that I began to think he hadn't heard my question, but then, with a smile on his face, he uttered one word: 'Incineration.'"

Not all his recollections of his student days were frivolous, however. He conveyed his struggles with split infinitives and dangling participles and his early confusion over metaphor, so easily used to excess. He taught his students how to moderate the use of metaphors so that they would be effective weapons rather than two-edged swords. While his students laughed at his recollections of his youthful indiscretions, they were learning to avoid those same pitfalls themselves. "All right, David," he would exclaim, directing his remarks at a lounger in the back row. "What is wrong with this sentence: He threw his eyes around the room and nailed them on the door?" And David would gather himself together and address the egregious mixing of metaphors.

Such was the force and ingenuity of Dr. Millstein's imagination that his students had to race to keep up with him. But no matter how difficult they found this challenge, somehow they always managed to succeed and, in the process, wrote more readily, more intelligibly, and more accurately. After twenty years of teaching, Professor Millstein was able to produce a long list of former students who had gone on to careers in writing, because he imagined them as professional writers long before any of them had learned from him how to write an intelligible and error-free sentence.

✑ Compassion

In conversations concerning professional behavior, discussions of feelings are often dismissed as improper. Yet it is impossible to understand teaching without acknowledging the chief emotion that prompts and motivates it when it is at its best—a profound concern for students that springs from the heart as well as from the head, an irresistible desire to help the young overcome their natural weaknesses and to dispel all people's ignorance. A remarkable teacher, one of the greatest the world has ever known, broke down and wept when brought face to face with the confusion and unhappiness that afflicted those who came to hear his teachings. "When he saw the multitudes," Matthew reports of Jesus, "he was moved with compassion on them, because they fainted, and were scattered abroad, as sheep having no shepherd."

When asked what they do for a living, teachers often describe themselves as promoting or professing particular subjects: "I teach English" or "I teach tenth-grade Latin." Yet these expressions are elliptical. What the teachers mean is that they teach English to undergraduates or Latin to tenth-grade students. The best of them have chosen their profession not necessarily because they have great affection for adolescent youth, but because they believe that the language or science they teach is important to the development of other, usually younger, minds and because they feel able to impart certain kinds of knowledge to the students in their classes. There is in the best teachers a profound enthusiasm for conveying their subject matter, a zeal which is almost missionary in intensity, which frequently makes every effort they make to do so exciting— to teachers themselves as well as to their students. Compassion in teaching is therefore not simply affection; it is an emotional reaction to the ignorance of the young, which creates in teachers a desire to wrestle with ignorance, substitute knowledge, and establish order and certainty wherever students' intellectual chaos and doubt are evident. Thus compassion is the basis for the necessary patience of teachers; no matter how inept or clumsy students' attempts at grasping the material may be, compassion ensures that teachers, rather than being scornful or condescending, will be tolerant and understanding.

The word *compassion* is appropriately used to describe these attributes of teaching because it connotes experience as well as sharing. The original Latin components of the English word mean "suffering with." Compassion is therefore inherent in teaching because teachers share with their students a sense of frustration, regret, and pain at the difficulties and struggles they must undergo to learn. It is not that students feel the same emotion but rather that their teachers remember the difficulties they experienced as students and are moved by that recollection. Those who have forgotten how hard it was to attain their achieved levels of mastery in a discipline will never be successful or happy instructors. The finest piano teachers remember their early struggles with their first five-finger exercises, the torment of the scales, and the stage at which the mere thought of playing anything that had more than three sharps or flats in a key signature prompted despair. That kind of summoned memory enables compassionate teachers to go through elements of instruction over and over again without the experience becoming stale or boring to them. The difference of one such experience from another, of course, is in the students, who are never the same, except in their difficulties and perplexities. Compassionate teachers therefore repeatedly "suffer with" their students.

Without this sense of common experience, no matter how controlled, suppressed, or concealed it may be, there is no successful practice of the art of teaching. It is a gut-wrenching emotion, as Matthew related it was for Jesus. The word used in the New Testament Greek and translated as "moved with compassion" means literally "to eat the inner organs," a phrase similar to our expression "to eat one's heart out." Since the inner organs include the heart, the expression is used metaphorically to mean "to feel emotion, pity, or compassion." This is no light sensation or passing fancy; it is a powerful reaction to the awareness of the difficulties that afflict others. Teachers often know its results as emotional, sometimes physical, exhaustion.

But if it is so important—indeed, crucial—to effective teaching, how does compassion manifest itself in the classroom?

Compassion requires first that teachers know who their students are. Even such simple practices as learning the names of students or asking them to complete questionnaires about themselves on the first day of class is a step in this direction. It begins the process of discovering how each student differs from others, how their minds work, what their views and experiences are, what particular strengths and weaknesses each has.

Teachers who ignore such considerations will get to know only the problem cases and the overachievers in each class; the other students, most of whom fall between these two extremes, will believe that their teachers have little concern for them or interest in their development, and their work will reflect that belief.

Compassion demands an adherence to high standards. It does not imply a lowering of them or a failure to hold students to account. Quite the contrary: a teacher's compassion arises from understanding students' travails as they strive to meet the challenges the teacher has set for them. True compassion is the identification by one person with the difficulties of another— the acknowledgement, not the denial, of those difficulties. A teacher's responsibility is in fact precisely to set those difficulties before the students, to provide the goals, incentives, encouragements, and rewards that will enable them to overcome their ignorance or their momentary helplessness so that they will be able to know more.

The confusion of compassion with charity is one of the principal misunderstandings of contemporary teaching. Teachers show regard for their students by setting high, though always reasonable, standards, by holding students responsible for meeting them, and then by exhibiting compassion toward them as they struggle to meet those standards. Making the work easier for students by adjusting their expectations downward is not compassion but negligent condescension. A compassionate regard for students requires setting appropriately high standards in the students' own interest. It is only by challenging students that a teacher reveals true compassion—a determination to relieve them of the ignorance that exacts severe penalties from both students and society together. To become known by students as "tough, but fair" is one of the crowning achievements of teaching.

Compassion requires that teachers put themselves in their students' places. This imaginative act enables teachers to anticipate the difficulties and reactions of their students. "Although that is wrong, I understand why you are making that mistake. Let me explain why," is the statement of a compassionate teacher, who tries to imagine the problems each student faces in learning something. The effort to see the material through the eyes of the students, to get inside their minds so as to understand their confusions and desires, helps teachers anticipate their students' questions and thus show them that they understand and appreciate the difficulties the students are encountering. Often teachers can reveal compassion for their students' confusions by asking them to report any difficulties in completing an assignment; or, in personal conferences, teachers can elicit from students those misunderstandings or difficulties they fail to admit to when surrounded by their peers. Compassion also means that while teachers try to avoid criticizing their students' intellectual performance, they are also honest and fair in their evaluations of it and in reproving any misbehavior.

Compassion makes approval enjoyable and correction palatable. The carrot and stick approaches to teaching must be carefully balanced. Compassionate teachers know to what extent approval and correction are to be used, and they ensure that the critique of the work of an individual student in no way discourages or intimidates either that student or listening classmates. This is a matter of ethics, and compassionate teachers will do their utmost to reprove students only in confidential settings. To be praised in the presence of peers is a rich reward, but to be rebuked in public adds humiliation to reprimand, often out of all proportion to the fault itself. Good teachers correct their students, but always in such a way as to protect the students' dignity and self-respect.

Compassion requires avoiding favoritism. A teacher's compassion must be general and must apply equally to all students; compassionate teachers single out no one student for particular favor or criticism. Compassion as well as ethics therefore makes teachers fair in dealing with their students. A responsible teacher cannot treat all members of a class in the same way; there will always be some students who require more attention than others if they are to have any success at all and others who can learn without special consideration. While compassion requires a uniform level of concern and interest, it does not demand a rigidly equitable division of teachers' time among all students. What it does require is that no member of a class should be or feel neglected or excluded.

Often this means that a teacher will have to search out those students who, for various reasons, remove themselves from involvement with a class and its work. In almost every class there will be students who desperately want to ask their teacher for more attention and help but are fearful of stepping forward. It is a teacher's duty to find and help those students. Similarly, there will always be objectionable, impertinent, and rude students whose behavior will tempt teachers to succumb to sarcasm or hostility. Handling these students—distinguishing between the students and their behavior—is among the truest tests of compassion.

Compassion moves teachers to acknowledge their students' struggles. This avowed and exemplified act of identification with students makes teachers' demands bearable to those who are trying to learn from them. Few things impede students' learning more than teachers who seem dismissive of their difficulties or who diminish or deride their achievements. Although criticisms are necessary ingredients of all teachers' methods, praise and empathy must fill each classroom. Success in learning invites celebration.

Most teachers are superior to their students in age, experience, and learning; but teachers must beware of allowing that superiority to dominate their attitudes toward those who study with them. Instead of saying, "I find this easy. Why do you find it so difficult?" good teachers will say, "Yes, this is difficult. I had an awful time with it when I was learning it. But let me see if I can explain it to you so that you can find it a bit easier than I did." Then, when the students have grasped the concept, it will be time for praise: "I remember spending three weeks grappling with that, and you've managed it in four days. Well done!"

Compassion means acting as a whole person. This aspect of compassion distinguishes great teachers from merely effective ones. Compassionate teachers bring their full personalities to class and do not act as if they have left significant parts of themselves at home. They are professionals sufficiently mature to have emotional lives that embrace, undergird, and strengthen professional engagement. Those teachers who check their emotions at the classroom door are usually dismissed by their students as "cold fish" or "phonies." These are the automata who wrongly believe that discipline and control can be established and maintained only if they behave in a mechanical and unfeeling way. There are no people without emotions; but many people in their professional lives, confusing rationality with lack of feeling, consider feelings obstructive, unprofessional, or threatening to their authority and thus dispense with them altogether. That is an error. Teachers who display no emotions often silence the already introverted, reticent students who speak only when comfortable with a teacher. Teachers with no obvious signs of human feeling cannot establish that sense of comfort and security that is so necessary to creating a teaching environment that invites and encourages participation.

Compassion is evident in a steady devotion to each student's future. It ought to be a concentration on each student's best interests that sustains teachers as they face resistance from their students, directives from their supervisors, complaints from parents, and criticism from the community at large. This desire to serve each student's interests guides the best teachers through such trials and gives them the fortitude to stick it out day after day.

Compassion is the foundation of this devotion, whose strength springs from acknowledgement of how the teacher's own life has been enriched through knowledge and by the hard labor needed to gain it. That devotion does not lie in seeking students' ease. It lies in challenging them to work—and then alleviating one's own concern for the pain involved in their working so hard by acknowledging what they are going through. "No pain, no gain" should be the motto of the classroom as much as the sports field, with the teacher seeking to ease the difficulties of learning with caring attentiveness and thus to encourage students to persevere.

Anyone contemplating teaching as a profession should consider compassion as a measure of suitability. The physical and emotional toll exacted by teaching will be too much for those lacking it; better by far that they leave the care of the ignorant to those who find their difficulties and their hunger to learn innately compelling. Those who experience difficulty in accepting the place of compassion in the classroom, who resist the idea of sympathetic emotions, or who prefer their working lives to be exclusively intellectual should avoid teaching altogether and probably consider devoting themselves to less demanding occupations, such as politics or crime.

THE PROFESSIONAL LIFE of Harriet Stiles was gratifying enough for her. She had been a successful student, and her willing industry, combined with a certain standoffishness toward her classmates and contemporaries, had led her own teachers to think that she had the right stuff to make a good teacher. Her parents had also insisted that she train for a career in teaching; they had persuaded her that, married or not, she would always be assured of a reliable source of income by teaching and that, if they were to be blessed with grandchildren through her, it would be a great convenience to her to enjoy the same periods of leisure during school vacations as did her children. So young Harriet earned a degree in English, acquired the necessary certification in education, and quickly secured a teaching post. She wondered from time to time whether she had the aptitude, inclination, or taste for the kind of work that her elders had marked out for her. But independent thought was not her strong point. And, after all, there are many who have chosen their careers in life from slighter motives and with more irrelevant purposes.

While Ms. Stiles always clung to the illusion that she had made a wise decision, it was a decision whose benefits for her students were less certain. For she had little aptitude for teaching. She was articulate and had some enthusiasm for English literature, finding especially in poetry material for her romantic flights of fancy; but she had little in common with the youngsters with whom she was destined to spend much of forty years. She considered them rude and irreverent. Furthermore, they were the children of others and therefore, she was certain, had not enjoyed the advantages of upbringing from which she had always benefited and which, in turn, she had tried to pass on to her own children. It was as if she could not forgive her students for their ignorance and illiteracy. Far from challenging her to greater efforts, their deficiencies merely disappointed and discouraged her. And she never failed to make her disillusionment known to students, friends, and colleagues.

She therefore taught tenth-grade English as if her principal objective was to demonstrate not only her superior understanding of Shakespeare's plays but also her absolute faith in the power of the dramatist's verse to elevate the most barbaric and illiterate temperament to the lofty level of her own sophistication. She made no attempts to project herself into her students' hearts and minds; indeed, the mere thought of such a perversion of her firm conviction threatened to make her ill. Rather, she remained aloof and Olympian, unapproachable and impregnable.

At times, her remoteness led her to deliver herself of views bordering on inscrutability. She might not explain Shakespeare, but she certainly flattered him. To the perennial question "Why do we have to read this stuff, Ms. Stiles?" her inevitable retort was, "When you say 'stuff,' I presume you are referring to the deathless writings of William Shakespeare." Once that point was clarified, she usually punished the miscreant with a penalty fit for the crime: the student would have to stay after class and write out for her a hundred times "A proper respect for Shakespeare is the mark of an educated person." If more justification were sought—more being quite unimaginable to Ms. Stiles— she would wax eloquent on the virtues of the Bard of Avon in language so outmoded that she would have embarrassed the dramatist himself. Such obscure and prescriptive assertions discouraged further inquiry by her students; anyway, avoiding difficult questions was, in Ms. Stiles's experience, always the best policy. To such questions as "Who was Caesar's wife, and why did she have to be above suspicion?" she knew the answers, and she expected her students to know the answers, too, which many of them came to do. But the greater questions about ultimate purposes floundered like beached whales all over the shores of her classroom.

Each of her classes contained a handful of students willing to play the game her way in return for her approval and the high grade that went with it. They became adept at asking the right kinds of questions, giving the right answers, flattering their teacher with the right words. They were her favorites, the ones she called on most frequently and paraded as models before the less pliable and more independent of their classmates, who were instead the subjects of Ms. Stiles's tirades against ignorance and low taste.

It never occurred to her to try to think with the minds of those students who resisted her instruction and thus proved themselves different from herself. Not only was she incapable of envisioning their difficulties with Shakespeare and with her teaching of his plays, but she would have considered the effort to see Shakespeare from those students' perspectives irrelevant to her purposes. These purposes included getting through the working day without interruptions of any kind from her charges and keeping them busy with the memorization of definitions and stock explanations so that they would forever after "know" their Shakespeare.

Her dedication to hard, little facts, tiny nuggets of knowledge unearthed by her unerring sense of the irrelevant for the admiration of her students, was legendary. Poetry, for instance, was for her an arrangement of words representing figures of speech, and these she insisted that her students be able to identify and classify correctly; thus hendiadys, metonymy, anaphora, and litotes never escaped the treadmill of her defining faculties, nor did many of her students ever forget their meaning—no small triumph, she thought, over the refractory ways of the human mind.

What did escape her, however, was the dramatic magic of poetry—Caesar's bloodstained toga and his gaping wounds, the struggle between duty and ambition, the contradiction between the lure of liberty and the appeal of successful leadership, the suppression of self-interest in a patriotic cause, and the corruption of good men into petty thieves. The notion that *Julius Caesar* addresses major questions apposite to contemporary concerns in public and civic life had occurred to her, but she had no interest in her students' youthful conceptions of current events and thus never made the connection. She taught the play because she had been taught it in the tenth grade; to her it seemed as established and traditional as Shakespeare himself. Besides, the language was not so bawdy as that of *Romeo and Juliet,* and this saved her from her students' nervous giggling and earthy exchanges about anything with a sexual connotation. And so because what the play was really about eluded her, it remained a mystery to her students. In her classroom, literature was dead on arrival, and it was the consensus among her former students, when they gathered in class reunions and talked about her, that Ms. Harriet Stiles had killed it.

These class reunions were a test for her. Since she had never learned her students' names when they were in her classes, she could not be expected to remember them later. But their faces? One would have thought that those of the best scholars or the worst miscreants would have lodged with her and that she might inquire after their lives. Instead, with her usual aplomb, she would ask if they could still recite the titles of Shakespeare's plays, and only the hardiest would stand by to try.

But it should not be presumed from all this that Ms. Stiles was a total failure as a teacher. Parents rarely complained to the principal about her, and she maintained good order in class. While she was stiff and unbending, she probably offered no worse a model to her students than those of her colleagues who scorned order and thought that the ideal of a disciplined classroom, to say nothing of a disciplined mind, was outdated. So though not a popular or inspiring teacher, she was accepted as innocuous but dull and, like the weather, inevitable. One of her students seemed to characterize her perfectly: "I suppose she knew something about Shakespeare," he said, "but she never seemed able to share it with us."

⟋ *Patience*

WHEN SHAKESPEARE, in *Twelfth Night*, put patience "on a monument, smiling at grief," he characterized it as the ability to accept loss gracefully in a world of sadness and tragedy. He also called up the image of an inert and passive victim too weak to rise up from adversity, an image that survives in our current word for a doctor's client. Yet even if teachers sometimes suffer—from hard, undercompensated, underappreciated labor, or from students who do not learn quickly or well enough—and if they sometimes feel that they cannot drag themselves through another day of punishing work, the patience required of them is an active, not a passive, virtue. Persistence allied with a determination to help others learn, as well as a kind of resignation to the difficulties students face, requires endurance, equanimity, and tolerance in about equal measures. Patience is thus one of the elements of teaching—unlike learning and imagination— that necessitates restraint rather than release; it requires teachers to harness their frustrations and fatigue, and to keep a steady eye on what they hope will be others' understanding of what they teach. If there is a classic case of inexhaustible patience, it is that of Helen Keller's teacher, Anne Sullivan Macy, who never ceased to invent and hope and thus led her gifted student out of darkness and silence to a rich life of understanding and inspiration to others—a gift of unremitting devotion that gained its recipient worldwide renown.

Acquired through constant practice, patience enables teachers to suspend disappointment and frustration out of an understanding of the difficulties students have in catching on to what their teachers already know. If the young are by nature impatient and impetuous, it is all the more important that their mentors be imperturbable and judicious. It is teachers, after all, who are supposed to be persuasive exemplars of better and more mature behavior; it is they who must teach and explain the values and utility of prudence, balance, and self-control. Experienced teachers, for instance, resist the temptation to rush through subject material they know well, because their students, for whom most new material is strange and challenging, must have time to digest and comprehend it. Patience in teachers is their willingness to accept students' limitations in their efforts to acquire knowledge so that the students may sense that they have company in its pursuit.

Patience also allows teachers to bear with their students' misconceptions and misunderstandings. Errors, after all, provoke both teaching and understanding; patience helps to arm teachers against dismissing errors as lacking utility or as unworthy of discussion. Errors provide opportunities for teachers to extend their lessons, try out fresh approaches, offer additional illustration and establish a standard, albeit a negative one, against which students can measure their own progress and satisfy their aspirations to know.

Yet critical as is the teaching value of errors and mistakes, that value can come into being only through students' trust of their teachers—trust gained in good part by teachers' patience with and generosity toward their students' flounderings and confusions. If teachers treat mistakes as evidence of stupidity, if they forget that errors frustrate, often mortify, the very students who commit them, they risk creating an impassable barrier between themselves and their students. Will students try again to answer a question, solve a problem, or write an essay if the teacher is likely to be contemptuous of the effort or scorn them for failing to get it right? Teachers without the trust of their students are like actors without audiences—all show and no response.

If patience is one of the principal foundations of trust, it also bears a close link to industry and diligence, without both of which, as most students are likely sooner or later to learn, learning does not occur. A teacher's patience teaches students to strive and strive again to get something right, to have patience with their own difficulties. In this way again, patience provides an example of behavior that the best teachers are always trying to provide. Patient teachers do not expect any greater achievement from their students than those students are capable of; teachers should instead be satisfied with their students' gradually increasing maturity and growing awareness and should expect great leaps of neither—though how gratifying both are!

Of course, teachers are understandably impatient with those students who do not try to learn or who squander the gifts they may possess in frivolity, dissipation, or laziness. Yet who can be sure that what appears to be a student's indolence is not something else—say, a physical or emotional difficulty of some kind? Recalling their own youthful indiscretions or difficulties may temper teachers' frustration about their own students' unfortunate behavior. Teachers' candor about their own past failings and the reasons for their natural frustrations about their students' foolishness may go far to alleviate their own impatience and suggest to their students that its source is the teachers' desire that the students learn and that they learn for their own good.

All this being said, what does patience contribute to instruction?

Patience gives students time to learn. Let time be on the students' side. Patient teachers restrain themselves from accelerating their instruction where their material seems relatively easy to their students; instead, they hold to a steady pace, one consistent not only with the abilities of their students to comprehend and to master what they are studying, but also with the customary rate of a class. Such teachers, while moving toward the goal of their students' comprehension of a subject, pause or backtrack when they find students unsure of the material they have already covered. Yet if a single student is having particular difficulty, these teachers try to find time for one-on-one coaching outside regular class hours rather than detain the entire group by addressing that student's needs in class sessions.

Patient teachers also extend themselves without complaining that additional effort may be unpaid work or that the extra work is not part of their professional obligations. Is this not, some will wonder, asking too much of teachers already burdened by the characteristic importunings of students, demanding hours of preparation, administrative duties, and their own lives, of which teaching is but one part? While it may be unjust to expect uncompensated work from everyone, teachers accept the responsibility of extra work when they take up their calling. The graceful acceptance of necessary tedium is one of the marks of great teaching, for it is really a gift of time, without which no student can learn.

Patience takes into account the weaknesses of youth. Those weaknesses are many, and often not fetching, yet they exist. If students are silly and giggle without provocation, if their spirits sometimes overcome their intellectual powers, if they occasionally forget themselves and the respect due to their teachers' authority—before all this teachers must nevertheless restrain themselves, count to ten, wait for their fit of impatience to pass, and then, in the calm that usually follows, point out to their students without rancor the foolishness of their behavior. Teachers are themselves foolish if they expect students to behave prudently and with discretion at all times. Even inappropriate behavior can itself be turned to good use with restrained indignation. "Now, Nathaniel, you've interrupted the class for half the period by making fun of George Washington for standing up in his boat while crossing the Delaware. And we've had enough of it. But you're right: the painter has painted him doing something that's never a good idea to do. Why do you think the painter has done so? What impression of Washington does it leave, and why do you think the artist wanted to leave that impression?" And off goes the lesson toward a serious end.

Patience hopes for, assists the growth of, but does not anticipate maturity in students. An old adage has it that you cannot put an old head on young shoulders. But there are occasions when teachers find themselves expecting from students qualities of character and intellect that should rather be expected from those who are older. The best advice to them is: Don't. If students are immature, teachers do not help them become mature by being impatient with them. Instead, a bit of well-meaning dissembling is probably in order, by which teachers act as if they sympathize with and will tolerate their students' immaturity in return for the required amount of work and progress on their part. What cannot be corrected, as the poet Horace remarked two thousand years ago in his *Odes*, becomes more tolerable with patience. To which one might add that what teachers pretend to tolerate now may prove to be correctable later.

Patience suffers fools gladly. That same ancient writer also noted that it is pleasant to play the fool in the proper setting. Students, especially young ones, are not likely to understand, at least at first, why classroom fun must be limited to an appropriate context—one determined by the teacher. It is teachers who must distinguish between foolishness that does not distract from learning and the kind of folly that is directly opposed to it. The latter should not be tolerated under any circumstances in a classroom. But harmless fun, the kind generated naturally by the effervescence of youth, is not likely to harm the pursuit of knowledge and may even smooth the way toward it. The challenge to teachers is to channel youths' natural ebullience into the search for knowledge without dampening their curiosity and fun.

Patience must be exemplified by teachers. Much is taught by example, and patience in a teacher contributes greatly to that effect. Where else will students find better models of fortitude, tolerance, and equanimity than their teachers? Generally we may hope that they will find such models in their parents and older relatives. Yet if not there, teachers may be the sole exemplars of forbearance that many youths meet; their teachers may be the only ones who can explain quietly the benefits of restraint or deliberation. They may be among the very few people whom students observe making use of those prudential qualities when they teach, counsel, and console. From time to time, therefore, teachers will find it appropriate to explain their own patient behavior, how they arrive at it, what they try to do when they are failing to maintain it, and the cost they have paid when they have acted without restraint or thought. Models need be neither mute nor perfect.

Patience never loses sight of the goal. Keep your eyes on the prize, in the words of the old gospel song. In this case, the prize is students' understanding, and excellent teachers move deliberately and steadily toward it. They allow nothing to distract or deter them from doing so. They know that the journey will be long and that they may be able to help their students only part of the way. Yet their escort, encouragement, and guidance must be unfailing while their students are in their trust. They then pass their students on to other teachers, often cheering them off to college, professional school, or career. And if they do so with sadness, it is sadness tempered with satisfaction and knowledge that they have taught their students well by making their best effort to expand the students' knowledge and understanding.

Patience gives rewards to the self. Rarely are teachers free of the sense that they might have had greater successes with their students, that their teaching skills ought to have been better, that they should have known more or been more understanding of their students' difficulties. And they are probably always justified in thinking so, if only because there is always room for improvement. Yet blaming themselves for their students' failure to learn can also hazard their success as teachers. A depletion of self-confidence only risks anxiety and diminished effect; and displays of that, to their students or colleagues, only undermines others' confidence in them and in their work. It is not that teachers are without responsibility for their deficiencies. But it helps to remember that much responsibility for their students' learning and maturing lies with others—when students are young, with their parents; when they are older, with themselves and their peers. So, also, it is always within teachers' powers to tackle their own perceived deficiencies with more study, more practice, more reliance on advice from their colleagues.

In general, all teaching is an exercise in patience. Sometimes it is our students we must endure; at other times, it is ourselves, as a strict grammarian might remark, up with whom we have to put. We wish that our students would move on, and we want to move them on, too. But that desire is often more a reflection of our hopes than of our students' true situation. They struggle, they are confused, they are not prepared to move forward. So we harness our hopes to their condition.

By doing so, however, we need not surrender hope to reality. What is patience, after all, but the triumph of faith and hope over despair? When we feel hopeless about our students' foolishness or willfulness, we may recall the existential determination of one of the characters in Samuel Beckett's *The Unnamable*—"I can't go on, I'll go on"—and, with tenacity, keep to our task.

⟨⟨⟨

ELSIE PLUNKETT taught social studies in an inner-city secondary school. Her students were in various states of desperation and need. Disadvantaged economically and socially, of many ethnic origins, they had only one thing in common: they all approached school as the last chance to escape from the poverty, disorder, and crime that surrounded the rest of their lives. Ms. Plunkett understood this well because of her own modest origins in Detroit. Nor had she forgotten the long struggle she had waged to improve her lot through education and take her place among other professionals. This much she had in common with her students, and, confident of the relevance of her experience to their lives, she related it to them without boastfulness or any hint of inverted snobbery.

Elsie Plunkett was one of those teachers who is determined to attend to her students' needs, whatever they might be and regardless of the cost to her time, temper, and professional advancement. Her tenacity was coupled with an equanimity of temperament that conveyed her confidence that her unsteady and uncertain students had the ability, with hard work, to get ahead. They discovered in her a model that was, for many of them, unique to their experience; they saw that she was effective and successful because of it, and they emulated her.

She used her classes as models for the society at large. We must tolerate each other's differences, she told her students, so that we can work together in peace and harmony; if we wish the rights guaranteed to us by the Constitution, she reminded them, then we must be willing to extend to others the same rights. Many in the room were themselves the victims of prejudice, which had embittered them in their relations with others of different races and places, and Ms. Plunkett was obliged to point out repeatedly that, when they indulged in expressions of particularistic scorn, they themselves were guilty of prejudice. Many of them had difficulties with English, bringing foreign accents to its pronunciation and confusion to its idioms. Because of this, not in spite of it, she insisted, quietly but firmly, that everyone should have a fair chance to speak and be heard attentively. Errors in speech she explained and corrected without reprimand; and though she was employed to teach social studies and not English, she was quick to praise any special effort to use sophisticated words and phrases correctly. Her classroom discussions were so disciplined and balanced that they formed a natural example of freedom of speech in action, and in this way the style and content of her teaching overlapped. Similarly, the concept of benevolent despotism, when they studied its meaning and history, was not hard for her students to appreciate with a living form of that kind of government standing before them.

In explaining the workings of society to her young charges, Ms. Plunkett kept to a steady pace so as to allow them ample time to absorb and retain the material. She went over difficult matters twice, often three or more times, probing and testing to make sure that every student was with her. When repetition failed, she would try again, slowing down the customary pace even further. If there were students who still could not keep up after that, she would arrange extra sessions on her own time to help them. The time she was ready to spend on any topic in the course extended to every student a fair opportunity to master it, no matter how long it took. And at the end of the process, her temper was as even and unruffled as it had been at the start. They found it hard to believe, but no student ever witnessed exasperation or heard an angry complaint from her.

In her classroom, she exemplified a major concern of the Constitution—how power is exercised, and by whom, in resolving conflict within societies—by the way she directed it. She moderated the conflicts in debate that arose out of the ignorance and inexperience of most of her students by her calm demonstrations of the strengths and flaws in their arguments, pressing them for facts and logic, explaining to them the authority of persuasion as compared with that of force. In this way she revealed the power of knowledge and experience, and her students learned that the best organized societies are those in which reason and civility hold sway.

Yet her classroom was not all grim toil. Ms. Plunkett had a playful sense of humor, which revealed itself in whimsical interpretations of the more obscure terms of political science. She could make jokes and invent puns and could enjoy both the wit and the silliness of her charges in return. Because difficult and unfamiliar terms like *bicameral, despot,* and *plutocracy* usually puzzled her students at first, she knew that she could fasten such essential concepts more securely in their minds every now and then with nonsense rather than cold definitions. She would explain that Congress was said to be bicameral because its two houses required at least two committees to decide to buy cameras for the Air Force—and they were always overpriced. She also pointed out that a plutocracy was not a Mickey Mouse form of government.

But not all her students were willing to devote themselves to learning with as ready a spirit as she wished. She knew firsthand the problems and threats they faced daily in their homes, on the streets, and even in the corridors of the school itself. For these reluctant and withdrawn souls her patience was a perpetual torment. She stuck to them like glue, pestered them with questions and encouragement, and allowed them no peace. She refused to give up on them, as many of their other teachers had done, and they quickly came to the conclusion that it was much easier to cooperate with her than it was to haul in the opposite direction. This was a tug of war in which the two sides were unequally matched—one woman, outweighed by her students and their environment, but outpulling them all the time. And as soon as any of them began to make efforts to follow her lead, she was quick with praise, her smile and encouragement more significant to them than any pleasure they may have gained from indolence. In this way there were no losers in her classes; and although their levels of achievement varied, all her students made progress toward the goal she set before them—a working mastery of the intellectual content of government along with a clearer understanding of their own and others' views of politics, the economy, and society.

⟡ Tenacity

THE QUALITY of tenacity has drawn the attention of writers and historians since ancient times. Think of Homer's Odysseus, determined, against almost insurmountable odds, to return home to his beloved Penelope. Think of the heroic figure described by a Roman poet: a person tenacious of purpose despite extraordinary odds, able to withstand a murderous mob intent on a lynching, a severe storm at sea, the frown of a cruel tyrant, the thunderbolt of great Jove himself, and the disintegration of planet Earth without flinching or fear of any kind. Closer up, think of nonfictional characters, like chattel slaves or prisoners of war, who have persevered, almost against hope, to maintain their very humanity in the face of outrageous conditions.

Of course, these are not the tribulations teachers normally face. But rare is the teacher who cannot summon recollection of trials that seemed almost as exacting to a committed professional as those, fictional and actual, who face threats to their lives: obdurate, undisciplined, uninterested, and weak students, parental intrusion, bureaucratic meddling, and political interference being only the most common of them. In the face of such obstacles, teachers understandably find it difficult to sustain a high sense of purpose. But unless they are to burn out or give up, they have to develop the capacity to stick to their work, to continually recommit themselves, and, as Thomas Jefferson once put it to John Adams, to steer their ship "with Hope in the head, leaving Fear astern." The barriers to instructional effectiveness cannot be allowed to make impossible what teachers know they can achieve under supportive conditions and with appropriate inner strength. But to achieve what they seek to achieve, they have to be tenacious.

The word *tenacity*, in its Latin origins, means no more than the act of holding or the ability to hold. Since ancient times, its usage has expanded so that the quality of tenacity is taken to be good and worthwhile as well as connoting strength. "We hold these truths to be self-evident," Jefferson famously wrote, in the avowal that made clear that the new nation was being launched from hard-won conviction and not from mere preference or opinion. His celebrated statement in the Declaration of Independence would have had little impact had it instead been phrased to read "We believe" or "We feel." "We hold" declares conviction and determination. There are no doubts. It puts every reader, every doubter, every opponent on notice.

Like so many of the principal elements of teaching, persistence in the face of countervailing realities is bound up with many of the qualities that the best teachers have to summon from within themselves each day without succumbing to self-doubt. Eventually, experienced teachers find that these inner resources somehow switch on as soon as they step into their classrooms; those resources become the attributes of personality and character that then characterize each instructor. But tenacity, like its near kin patience, may be the most difficult of any of the other elements of teaching to apply consistently, for it must always be applied in the same way in each situation and evenhandedly among all students. Few elements require what is really an application of will—the will to be equitable while unrelenting, to have more confidence in students than the students themselves possess. No demand on teachers makes clearer than tenacity that being in a classroom, like being on the playing field, is not for the fainthearted. In fact, athletics provide a useful metaphor for persistence; for whether in practice or competition, players and their coaches must somehow combine self-discipline, hope, and determination to develop the talent a team—that team being both coach and players, all with the same mutual goal—needs to find satisfaction in a sport and to succeed at it. Tenacity is like an automobile's fuel; it is not seen, but without it the car goes nowhere.

Tenacity is the quality that lies somewhere between patience and obstinacy. It is neither passive resistance nor mindless aggression. It holds to what is needed—which, for teachers, should be what is true and good—with a firmness that never relents. Passive resistance can turn into a kind of martyrdom, and obstinacy is a mark of bigotry and intolerance. By contrast, to be tenacious in teaching is to cling to the highest expectations of self and students. It demands a toughness of mind and spirit that is the very stuff of heroism, even if teachers do not risk their lives in the line of duty. Moreover, if applied right— veiled by teachers, yet sensed by students—it offers students an example of how firmness can be combined with grace.

As with all elements of teaching, the exemplary role of firmness cannot be overlooked. Without pointing it out to students, teachers have to be models of the very characteristics they are trying to instill in those they teach. Sometimes, what they teach can be made the avowed models of perseverance. Who can learn of the efforts of Elizabeth Cady Stanton and Susan B. Anthony, Thurgood Marshall and Martin Luther King, Jr., without being struck by those people's perseverance? As the examples of their lives and efforts illustrate, doggedness often fits snugly with the people to whom it is applied as well as with the person who possesses and embodies it. It is both *of* self and *for* others. Stanton and Anthony, Marshall and King were firm in conviction and behavior so that others would remain firm, too. All, we would say, were tenacious. They knew in their bones the rightness of what Winston Churchill once urged an audience: "Never give in—never, never, never!"

But how can teachers not get discouraged from simply thinking about what they must summon of unyielding determination when faced with the students they are given to teach?

Tenacity means, above all things, an acceptance of discouragement. To face students day after day, year after year, requires the application of hope to the possibility of failure. One of the realities of instructing any group of people is that teachers often cannot learn whether they have succeeded in getting their students to know and think better than they did because of the teaching they received. Learning rarely makes itself known immediately; it is cumulative and is likely to become apparent only after students have left their classrooms behind. So teachers, often never seeing their students again and having to depend on confidence that they have done some good, can easily conclude in the absence of much concrete evidence that they have failed to get through to their students however much they may have tried. Teachers can surely take satisfaction in having simply made the repeated, often unrecognized and unacknowledged efforts called for to teach others. But they must also take solace in the possibility that their endeavors are probably working out of sight in the mind and character of those they have taught. Faith that this is so constitutes the foundation of all that teachers do. To surrender that faith is to surrender to hopelessness, and hopelessness marks the dissolution of the tacit bond between teacher and student.

Tenacity must be visible while unstated. No purpose is served by telling students that you plan never to leave them alone in trying to find ways to help them learn. They must experience their teachers' steadfastness simply as a quality that teachers possess; they needn't know that most teachers are likely to have struggled to develop and maintain an indefatigable composure in the face of the obstacles that students can constitute. In spite of students' refractoriness and the variety in their abilities and willingness to learn, one must summon optimism to confront and overcome often discouraging reality. Students can feel a teacher's singleness of purpose without ever being told what the teacher is up to. Like most of the contents of a teacher's collection of qualities, resolve is best when unspoken and just there.

Tenacity calls for unremitting, often unrequited, effort, but it never justifies anger toward students for their failure to live up to their teachers' hopes or expectations. This may be among the most demanding of all teachers' duties—to keep at work without apparent results and without anger. One will occasionally feel like lashing out at refractory students or at those who are not quick of mind; equally tempting may be, in the spirit of medieval flagellants, to turn inward to self-recriminating scourges. Both responses to frustration have to be firmly resisted. Anger, unless for gross misbehavior, has no legitimate place in classrooms; self-recrimination simply does no good. So what can be done in the face of discouragement? Steely discipline of self is really the only answer—discipline to persevere in the face of often intractable odds. There is no other option that does not compromise a teacher's basic commitment to students' welfare or, alternatively, does not require giving up teaching altogether. Yet persistence in the absence of evident gains in students' knowledge is a distinct quality. Teachers' commitment to their students' best interests must sustain them come what may. This is no less demanding an act of faith than a religious one; both call for imagining what might be in the best of worlds but that does not yet exist.

Tenacity makes burnout unlikely. "A strenuous soul," wrote Ralph Waldo Emerson, "hates cheap successes." Teachers who hate cheap successes, who at the end of the day can say that they did their best, are more likely to sustain their commitment to students than those who seek discounted gains. The private satisfaction of having lived up to one's own standards when those standards have benefited others is beyond measure. Teachers who can say that they have gone the full distance are unlikely to give up. For such people, easier kinds of work will have no appeal. They will not be challenging enough.

Tenacity keeps teachers from giving up on difficult, indifferent, or failing students. Teachers' responsibilities require them to help their students attain results—to gain knowledge and understanding—beyond the expectations of both. Every class is likely to have students who try to succeed and do so beyond the general level of the rest. Every class is also likely to contain students who try and fail and those who neither try nor succeed. These are the ones that call for unremitting application on a teacher's part. Some willingly try, but their capacities are modest, and their needs are great; everything must be repeatedly explained to them, and they need repeatedly to review what they have recently learned. Students who never try to learn are the most difficult, for if they do not try, how will they learn? No harder cases test the endurance of their teachers. Yet for all the teachers' efforts, the yield is likely to be slim.

That being the case, are teachers expected to be exempt from discouragement over their failure to move such students ahead? Surely not. Yet they cannot allow themselves to be daunted. Their responsibility—and it is an ethical one, too—is not to succumb to their discouragement but instead, by trying consistently and cheerfully to overcome the challenges such students pose, to keep at it in the hope that these toughest of all students will eventually make some progress if only for the very fact that their teachers are unrelenting.

Tenacity means maintaining high standards—for self as well as for students. Rare is the teacher who, at one time or another, is not tempted to reduce standards and expectations in order to get respectable results at a lower level of achievement. That temptation differs from accepting results from students who do not reach the level of attainment that teachers set for them, an everyday affair in all classrooms. But teachers have to remind themselves frequently that the standards they set are set for their students' benefit, not their own ease; for their students' acquisition of knowledge, not for test scores that will make the teachers look good. Keeping standards a bit ahead of their students' current reach is bound to result in some students falling short and therefore in teachers', as well as students', discouragement. But considered in the right light, students' shortcomings are simply an artifact of teachers' expectations. Consequently, teachers always do the right thing in applying the carrot rather than the stick.

Furthermore, for students all expectations are standards. Low expectations make a subject or course the well-known laughing stock of every school and campus—the "gut" course. A faculty member known as "A. B." Jones for giving high marks to everyone registered in his course is no adornment to a campus or a help to any students genuinely seeking to learn that ancient tongue. On the other hand, standards set too high can keep away from courses students who might greatly benefit from and enjoy them. It is no easy task to set standards just right—for any particular population of students at any stage of their studies. But finding a way to do so, making them clear, adhering to them consistently, and being fair in their application has to be one of the surest routes to success as a teacher.

In the face of obstacles and setbacks, teachers have to remind themselves constantly what they are seeking to achieve. Faced with different students for years on end, they soon discover that, sure enough, taken as a whole each group is roughly similar to the ones that have preceded it—composed of the same range of human characters with the same range of human gifts and weaknesses. To add to this reality is the bald fact that while all courses are new for the students taking them, they can be old stuff for the teachers leading them, even if their lesson plans or lectures change. The challenge always is to accept this reality as a stimulant, not a burden, and thus to stay fresh and draw something rewarding from each effort, even if repeated. Each course, for each teacher, is another episode in the cooperative search for knowledge and understanding.

Tenacity is called to duty at every stage of these efforts—for students as well as for teachers. But teachers face by far the heaviest burdens for they have the heaviest responsibilities and must constantly resummon their commitment to one of the hardest jobs on earth. Each teacher must uniquely figure out how to do so; each must discover how to find the energy to face each class and somehow to help others learn—through command of a subject, humor, understanding, and the tricks of the trade that compose this, as every other, calling. Adherence to that commitment to others' learning can, under the many trying circumstances that face teachers, sometimes wane. But steadfastness of purpose and hope is likely always to carry the day.

❦❦❦

"Oh, man," came the complaint. "Not more free throws?" "Yep. Get on with them," Coach Thompson pushed back. "This isn't for me, pal. It's for you guys. You think I don't want to call it a day, too? But how can we win the championship if we don't keep at it?"

William Thompson had been coaching boys' basketball at Thomas Paine High School for seven years. He was a stranger neither to fatigue nor to discouragement. The talent he had to work with each season, like sand in northern California rivers, rarely yielded gold nuggets. But his responsibility was to take his "raw material," as coaches like to call their players, and turn them into serviceably skilled athletes, perhaps even into championship contenders. This year, he seemed to be closer to that goal than ever before.

His players were a typical unruly adolescent lot of boys: irrepressible, irreverent, hard to herd. Like him, they came from unpromising backgrounds—divided families, a poor community—and had been denied much that the world holds out to others. Coach Thompson saw himself in them; and he did his best to give them the inner discipline that his parents had imparted to him. It was tough going. Only two hours a day with those eighteen boys: the chances of making much of a difference to them were slim. And he had to do it through athletics, not classroom teaching. That meant without the spur of grades or the threats of classroom discipline. Instead, it had to be by example and hope—both backed up by more steely determination than his boys yet possessed.

Coach Thompson saw himself as a teacher, one in league with his colleagues in the nearby classrooms, all focused on developing thinking adult citizens. His players saw him as a tough disciplinarian. They knew that he was on their side and wanted them to win games as much as they did. What they did not know was that, for him, practice and play were means to an end, not ends in themselves. Winning was not everything; learning was. Trying to learn how to win was the goal.

"So let's try again," he said—an order couched as a plea. "Dwayne, you're still raising your right hand too high. Franklin, don't bend your knees so much." And thus it went for another fifteen minutes, until everyone was wrung out. "Let's call it a day."

Thomas Paine High School was distinctive in considering its coaches to be part of the teaching faculty. Whether or not they taught courses, they taught. Coach Thompson had been trained as a science teacher. But since he was also known to have been a star athlete in his youth, the school had asked him to take over a losing basketball program. "Only if I can continue to teach biology," he insisted. So half his responsibilities remained in the classroom. He wanted his students to attain merit scholarships as much as he wanted his players to win games. This year, however, the latter was proving more difficult.

"Look, guys," Coach Thompson started off the next practice. "You're terrific at layups and outside shots. But many games are won or lost at the free throw line. So we're going to practice only those again today—over and over and over again until you get it right." "Oh no," came the chorus. "Not again!" "Yes, again. Are you here just to have fun, or do you want to win games and take the trophy this year? I'm fine with your just having fun, but you guys don't seem to be having any. We won't have a chance of winning the league unless we keep at it. So which is it, fun without work, or hard work for the satisfaction of having tried your best even if you don't win?" The question answered itself.

At the school's next faculty meeting, Coach Thompson gave his colleagues the names of his players. "Don't let up on them, please, but also know that they're under strain these days. They've got to learn to persevere in everything. I can only ask that you all help them do so. That's my goal, too."

He was never certain that his approach was working. Some of his boys wanted to give up; others didn't follow his directions. Two got into a fight. "I'm not sure we're getting anywhere," he confided to a colleague. "I try and try and try, but we don't seem to get better."

That may have seemed so, but his team began to win games anyway. Some team members took this as permission to let up in practice. "Not on your life," was the coach's response. "No slacking off for any of us, you or me. We're going to keep pushing ourselves until each of us can say we did all we could."

They did. At the end of the season, they eked out a win in the final game and clinched the league title. The score? 73–70, won by three free throws.

"You guys kept oh-man-ing me, trying to get me to cut back, 'til I didn't want to hear the word 'man' again. But what good would have cutting back done? Without my prodding, you might not have won the championship. What lesson do you take from this?"

"OK, Coach," came the reply. "We get it. Never give up. Never!"

↝ Character

TEACHERS OF PREVIOUS AGES, both in legend and in history, often had forbidding temperaments. Severity was a common mark of their personalities, and descriptions of eighteenth- and nineteenth-century classrooms frequently portray schoolmasters as inflicting corporal punishment on their unfortunate students with a cane, switch, or ruler. In "The Deserted Village," Oliver Goldsmith depicted one such teacher as "a man severe . . . stern to view."

> I knew him well, and every truant knew;
> Well had the boding tremblers learn'd to trace
> The day's disasters in his morning face.

Few are now likely to be Goldsmith's "man severe." Today's successful and admired teachers are more likely to be noted for their congeniality, good humor, and tolerance than for their harsh discipline and scowling looks. This does not mean that they are usually playful clowns—they must not be—but it does mean that the misanthropic sourness connoted by the profession of teaching in the past is rarely found now. Teachers' personalities, or so conventional views have it, should be at least attractive, if not charming. After all, it was with music and the eccentric costume of a jester that the Pied Piper made all the children of Hamelin follow him.

Yet one cannot fashion personality, as one can character; teachers ought to bring to their work themselves, not some manufactured personas. The challenge of personality that confronts them is not that of making themselves pleasing to their students, as much as that may seem to be desirable, but that of drawing out of themselves the traits of character—the traits of their moral nature—that will accommodate and enhance their students' learning. There are always a few unsuccessful teachers who manage to reach at least a few of their students despite some annoying trait of personality, such as the lack of any sense of humor or play. And there are the gifted and inspiring teachers who nonetheless fail to reach some students because, given the mysteries of the fit of human personalities, the students simply do not learn well from those particular teachers. Who is therefore to say that for one teacher a severe approach to learning, or for another a gently persuasive mode of instruction, is wrong or inappropriate? All teachers must consider how they can use the mental and moral qualities that are inherently theirs to best effect in the classroom. No exposure to methods, no practice of technique, can substitute for that.

A trap young teachers often fall into is that of assuming "teaching personalities" that are not their own. Such teachers are like unconscious actors; they are playing roles based, often unknowingly, on the favorite schoolteachers or college mentors of their own youth. Acting may be an important technique of successful teachers, but the adoption of roles must always be deliberate and temporary—and always for good effect. Teachers who assume permanent masks without realizing what they are doing are guilty of a kind of hypocrisy particularly offensive to the young, who show a remarkable talent for unmasking such deceptions. The classroom is not a stage, and those who feel obliged to assume different characters in order to be effective in it should probably not be teachers in the first place.

A prime example of such a teacher is Andrew Crocker-Harris, the pathetic if gentle character of Terence Rattigan's stage drama *The Browning Version*, who has over many years assumed a personality of such ruthless coldness that his students call him "the Hitler of the Lower Fifth" behind his back. Yet on the eve of his retirement a student reduces him to tears with the gift of a secondhand copy of Robert Browning's translation of the *Agamemnon* of Aeschylus. Difficult though it may be to believe, this appears to be the first time in a forty-year career that Crocker-Harris has revealed anything of his true personality in the presence of his students. Yet the playwright persuasively portrays a teacher brought to the verge of nervous breakdown by a lifetime of deliberate deception through denial of himself.

If there is an ideal character for a teacher, it is one occupying a middle position between conflicting extremes. To be kind is not to be soft or weak, and to be demanding is not to be unfair. The balance to be achieved lies with a good-natured reserve and an enthusiastically generous sharing of intellectual excitement; such a balance keeps teachers from corrupting the appropriate relationship between themselves and their students.

The personal qualities required of successful teachers are not difficult to identify. Whether they are acquired or are the gifts of nature are questions best left to geneticists to consider. Intelligent young people are often urged to consider careers in teaching by those who observe in them the traits they suppose to be required in good teachers: consideration for their peers, for instance, or kindness toward those in need of help with their studies. Those attracted to teaching careers merely by their interest in a particular subject or a sense that teaching is the only way they can be paid for indulging in it are likely to experience difficulty in the classroom, possibly failure and unhappiness, because their personalities may be quite unsuited to their work.

A teacher's age and each generation's accompanying changing traits of character are also factors in teaching. Teachers of twenty-three may have to face classes of eighteen-year-olds, who are apt to consider their young instructors as older siblings. In front of such a class, there is little point in attempting to play the graybeard. Fifteen or twenty years older, teachers may well be thought of as substitute parents. Still later, if the years have been kind, the role of a grandparent will probably be appropriate before young students. Maintaining a suitable distance between teacher and student at each of these stages in the teacher's aging requires an appropriate maturing of personality. In turn, teachers must resist the illusion that the aging process affects only the students, who seem to get younger every year.

Yet there is no single, ideal character for teachers. Human types being infinitely varied, many very different kinds of character can "work" in a classroom. Thus this element of teaching is particularly difficult to define. But it does have some generally common features.

A teacher's teaching character must be authentic. Just as the ancient Greeks advised "Know thyself," so the first rule of teaching is "Be thyself." Teachers who are casual, informal, and gentle by nature should not present themselves to their students as rigid, disciplined, and severe; those who are naturally serious and laconic should not practice being light-hearted and loquacious. All teachers ought to accept their own natural traits and strive to make them work in the classroom for the benefit of their students. Perfection is not required of a teacher, but naturalness is.

Good teachers possess enough self-knowledge to develop and use those qualities of their personalities, both "good" and "bad," that work for them in different classrooms. Knowledge or technique ungrounded in character is of little effect with students; on the other hand, knowledge anchored to a teacher's irrepressible passion for a subject, or technique linked with personal experience, attracts and gives assurance to students. What teachers bring to their classrooms from their own lives outside is an essential part of themselves that should not be kept from their students if it promotes learning.

Character must be consistent. Good humor, equanimity, and friendliness are qualities students expect of their teachers at all times. Demanding as that expectation may be, it is not unreasonable; students learn best when their teachers' bearing is stable and can therefore be taken for granted. There is little room for greatly varying shifts of mood or for anger, disappointment, or despair. These emotions may well afflict the personal lives of teachers, but they must be left at the classroom door. They cannot help students, and they have no bearing on the subject matter of a course. This is not an invitation to hypocrisy, but it does necessitate a firm control of personality for the greater achievement of professional character. For teachers, at least, some measure of stoicism is probably necessary.

Character means showing humanity by acknowledging lapses and errors. Authenticity and consistency of character ought not to imply faultlessness. They do, however, require honesty about those failures of knowledge and self that affect one's students. Although confessions about a teacher's personal problems have no place in instruction, apologies for short-temperedness occasioned by those problems will regain students' trust and may instruct through exemplary action. Moreover, any errors in teachers' presentations discovered after the fact must be admitted and corrected as soon as possible. No teacher is capable of knowing all the ways to present materials, and none should be expected to be. Yet since conveying accurate knowledge is one of the chief aims of teaching, errors of fact or interpretation must be candidly confessed, better methods than those previously used ought to be presented, and the significance of both should be explained. Not only is learning thus promoted and honesty exemplified, but perhaps more important, teachers themselves can be seen struggling to overcome the natural difficulties of learning, and their students can thus grow in understanding.

Character requires sociability. Teachers must find a balance between overfamiliarity and icy detachment. They should not be their students' closest friends, but students need to feel that their teachers are approachable and interested in their lives as well as their learning. All teachers on occasion dismiss students too abruptly when they could have helped them by being more patient and attending to their questions and concerns with greater care; and some go too far toward the other extreme and become too familiar with those whom they are trying to teach, when they ought to keep back and encourage their students to grow free of their influence. Constant vigilance against these all-too-human tendencies is of the greatest importance for teachers. The best of them will be readily available sources of counsel to their students where matters related to instruction and study are concerned, and they will respond to students' requests for advice of a more personal nature by being neither too involved nor too aloof.

Character should mature with age. At all stages in their working lives, teachers should try to become, as teachers, the people they are. It is a mistake for teachers to cling to personalities that suited their early twenties when they are in their middle forties, even though the conscious inclination to retain a particular trait that worked twenty years before is understandable. Teachers ought to feel free to allow their changing selves to enter the classroom, rather than retaining characteristics that were their authentic selves at an earlier stage in their lives but which no longer are so. Teachers who impersonate themselves at earlier points in their careers invite ridicule.

Character should be distinct and individual. To describe human personalities, the ancient Greeks used the term *character* to describe the impression made on coins and seals to convey both identity and value. This numismatic image of character may be applied appropriately to teaching, where we require the authentic and shun the counterfeit. Teachers' impressions on their students should be deep and sharp if character is to have some bite to it. For this reason, teachers are often regarded by the world at large as somewhat eccentric; we hear it said that they are "real characters." This should be to their credit, even if meant as a slur. For with real character is likely to come real teaching. Teachers who create a distinct impression on their students are more likely to lead them to real learning.

All these considerations can be reduced to one principle: do not play the role of someone you are not. Let your own character evolve into the teacher that you are most suited to be. We all have characteristics of personality that would be better conquered or at least moderated, especially when we are with a class. Sarcasm, facetiousness, selfishness, and laziness are common enough in all of us, but such traits often impede effective teaching. Therefore, such traits should be tempered—better, they should usually be suppressed—and a kind of purification process should occur as we step across the threshold from the corridor into the classroom. The medieval custom of having teachers wear academic dress whenever they were lecturing or teaching probably helped our predecessors in this way; it was hard not to behave in a proper and professional manner when clothed in a long black robe. Certainly, this habit was a continual reminder of the seriousness of the task at hand. Even if teachers have now doffed that kind of garb, those who follow other lines of work—be they priests, rabbis, ministers, judges, doctors, or police officers—dress for their particular work and no doubt adjust their psyches as they put on their robes and uniforms. By comparison, today's teachers lack such conventional props; their preparation must therefore be exclusively internal and unseen. This requires a greater concentration of will than the donning of special dress. It also necessitates an understanding of what aspects of character contribute to good teaching.

But above all things, developing an appropriate teaching character requires teachers to work hard to distill from their own personalities and experiences those dimensions of self which will most enhance their students' ability to acquire knowledge. Each teacher's way of doing so will be distinctive; the outcome of each teacher's search for the person consistently to be in the classroom will be unique. But in every case that search must be conscious. To avoid that challenge is to risk defeating the whole purpose of teaching.

☙☙☙

IT HAS BEEN SAID that cheerfulness will prevent any consistent study of philosophy, and too much humor may very well overwhelm any sustained effort to teach. Certainly this was true of Francisco Garcia, a fifty-four-year-old community college professor nominally responsible for teaching psychology. A large, jovial man with the body of a former linebacker and the disposition of Santa Claus, Professor Garcia was immensely popular with the young because of his relaxed attitude to life and his lively devotion to comedy. Many students classify teachers into two groups: those who tell jokes and those who do not. It was immediately obvious to them to which group Dr. Garcia belonged. Vaudeville and slapstick attained immortality in his classes; the cornier the joke or routine, the louder the laughter that followed it. The fact that most of the laughter erupted from the professor himself did nothing to deter him from continuing to exploit every conceivable opportunity for mirth, especially his innocent mother-in-law, who was continually abused for no good purpose.

Francisco Garcia was a stand-up comic in the classroom, always two jokes or two punch lines ahead of his captive audiences and scarcely aware of his listeners' reactions. What little psychology was covered during his monologues was introduced as both fun and funny, and students remembered his lectures either as a string of jokes or not at all. Most students accepted Professor Garcia as a campus character and a distinct contrast to other members of the faculty, most of whom were serious to a fault or at best sardonic in their humor; he by contrast amused them, they tolerated him, and the campus had a general sense that his was one class where expectations were low and little effort needed. Some students, a minority, resented Dr. Garcia intensely, found his teaching grossly inadequate, and thought his clownish antics insulting to their intelligence. Yet because they were in a distinct minority, these students felt guilty about the role of spoilsport that their professor's antics forced upon them.

Professor Garcia had discovered early in his career that getting a laugh out of students was much easier than teaching them psychology. It pleased him to reflect on how funny he seemed to most of his students; it made him feel that he was popular and well loved. The hostility of a few students, who would have preferred to learn more psychology and endure fewer bad jokes, did not trouble him. "There are always a few bad apples in any barrel," he would remind himself by way of consolation.

During lulls between witticisms, Professor Garcia would remind his students that they should have covered this or that chapter in the textbook by now. He would also tell them that if there was anything in the text that they did not understand, they should feel free to question him about it. In this way he "covered" the material, few questions were asked, and those that did arise he could as easily deflect with a joke as answer helpfully.

Students who posed questions to Professor Garcia not only felt that they were admitting ignorance in the presence of their peers; they also subjected their names to his endless capacity for puns or their physical appearance to public ridicule. One young man named Wood one day asked an innocent question about child development, only to be subjected to a monologue about going against the grain and barking up the wrong tree. Wood was also asked several times why he "would" ask such a question and told that, if his father had similar doubts at the same age, it would prove that he was a chip off the old block.

This conduct on the part of Professor Garcia might have jeopardized his career if his jokes had been anything other than merely silly; if his humor had descended to the obscene or scatological, it would surely have entangled him in difficulties with parents, administrators, and public officials. But he stayed out of trouble by avoiding religion, sex, and the earthier bodily functions in launching his wisecracks. His geniality naturally extended to his colleagues, and he was always willing to serve on committees, where he would make indignant speeches about the ineptitude of his students and their inability to absorb simple ideas in psychology. He would also wax eloquent on the poor preparation his students had received in high school and thus shift the responsibility for his own inadequate teaching onto the shoulders of unidentifiable predecessors. Many of his colleagues therefore believed him to be a brilliantly amusing teacher who unfortunately had blockheads for students.

Though Professor Garcia's classroom personality was comforting to him, he had no sense of what his students needed and no concern for their intellectual welfare. In the classroom, his principal object was to amuse himself, and the apparent amusement of others was the pleasant by-product of this preoccupation. Though he might have been better suited to the worlds of selling, advertising, or entertainment, his success in those fields would have depended on his ability to blame others for his defects and avoid detection in doing so, and he probably suspected that he would fail at both. So he remained a community college teacher.

If Professor Garcia had adopted a motto, it might well have been "Leave 'em laughing"; it certainly wouldn't have been "Leave 'em learning." But his early, successful experiences in the classroom had shown him how easy it was to be liked by the majority of students for telling jokes, and he had succumbed to the siren of popularity, his appetite for easy acclaim much stronger than his interest in teaching well. And that appetite had never abated throughout his career.

When he eventually retired from the college after more than forty years, he was lauded in the farewell ceremonies for what was described as his "dedicated service." He spent his golden years writing articles castigating his former colleagues and advocating the reform of teaching. While these writings lacked substance and authority, they had readers, as Francisco Garcia noted with great satisfaction, "rolling in the aisles."

≈ Pleasure

ALTHOUGH A FEW PEOPLE teach because it is the only way they can earn a living while engaging in their true love—like painting or carrying on research—most teachers teach because it gives them the deepest sort of satisfaction. And this is how it should be. It is difficult to imagine effective teachers who do not have an abiding fascination with their subjects, who do not love being among students, and who do not gain fulfillment from nourishing others' minds and lives. Most people who teach also do so in part because it involves plain good fun—laughter, humor, and wit. Teaching, that is, ought to bring and give pleasure of many kinds; it should be play as well as work. The classroom should be a place for light hearts as well as serious minds. It should be a place where knowledge is fastened to desire and where the passion for understanding is satisfied.

This may seem like heresy to classroom puritans, but it must be recognized that while the purpose of all learning and instruction is deadly serious, the paths to the mind, like those to the heart, are many and varied, and pleasure is one of the most direct. Who has not known students who learn because for some mysterious reason of their own they find a subject captivating? When a class masters a difficult subject, should not a teacher's spirits soar? And should not pride, admiration, and praise be among students' rewards for learning? If students and their teachers fail to experience feelings of joy, happiness, even occasional giddiness as they learn and develop together, then something is wrong.

At its very best, teaching is a form of intellectual play in which students are invited to join. Play for the purpose of learning asks students to bring to their learning the same traits of mind and spirit called for by all genuine play—delight in chance and the unexpected, concentration, inventiveness. Those who interpret play in the classroom—whether it takes the form of games, acting, debate, or contests—as the absence of seriousness are mistaken. As we know from watching young children playing games, their grave attention is in pursuit of fun. So, too, with the obverse: a teacher's sheer playfulness with students can be in pursuit of knowledge. Through joking, the surprises of sharp wit, or role playing, fun is in service to the broader aims of learning. After all, most laughter arises from recognition of truth. A teacher's laughter often means even more—an ease with a subject and mastery of it; and as theorists of comedy have pointed out, the variant of pleasure that we know as humor implies, indeed creates, openness to the possibilities of new understanding through fresh arrangements of words, ideas, and images.

The pleasure of teaching, then, is reciprocal: as teachers feel pleasure by giving it, students gain pleasure and return it by pleasing their teachers. Yet a teacher's greatest pleasure always arises from the students' achievements—from, say, their conquest of previously great intellectual challenges or from their distinctive and fresh combinations of ideas. Some teachers will become joyful as they witness their students gaining a skill; others will be delighted by their students' imagination. In all such cases, teachers feel pleasure because through their own gift of self they have enabled others to achieve something fresh, to enlarge their understanding, to be edified as well as instructed.

All of which suggests a cautionary note: that the pleasure of teaching and learning must always be directed at raising understanding and aspiration and should never come at another's expense; it must be in service to appreciation, not depreciation, and it should never be cynical. These are not injunctions easily met, for the taste of humor is often sweet when ridiculing and sarcastic. Yet laughter must never cost a student's self-respect; nor should it diminish the intrinsic integrity of something— be it a situation in the past, or a work of art, or a scholar's researches. An even more serious enemy to understanding is cynicism, a denial of wonder and play. Condemning our lesser ways without acknowledging our nobler nature, cynicism denies the kinds of distinctions that give knowledge and choice meaning; it implicitly suppresses analysis and exploration out of a know-it-all fatalism; worst of all, it implies that all human motives are base. Such attitudes are usually fatal to learning.

Not all teaching and learning can be interesting or fun; gaining and conveying knowledge often involves drudgery and, because difficult, is frequently exhausting. No good teachers fail to acknowledge that this is so, nor do they fail to make known uncomplainingly their own hard work. Teachers cannot expect to attract their students to learning through pleasure alone, because learning is laborious and demanding. But as every teacher knows, it is hard work applied to mastery of something that often attracts some students by the special pleasure and satisfaction it brings them.

So how can teachers ensure that they will be feeling pleasure as well as giving it?

Pleasure means creating an atmosphere in which students enjoy learning. This is not to suggest that all lessons, all learning, can or should be pleasurable; the most lasting gains in knowledge, the deepest understanding, arise from great toil. Yet when learning is tied to goals within students' extended reach, when it leads to what students themselves can see as an enhancement of their understanding of the world, when it gives them a glimpse into the mysteries of life, into new and alien realms of knowledge, then it leads to pleasures and satisfactions of the greatest sort. Learning then becomes infectious, and students will say in their engaging way that school is "fun."

Pleasure requires letting others' wit shine. As long as they are not employed at the expense of others, humor and fun are clarifying, relieving, and engaging. When it comes from the generous side of the spirit, humor ought to be encouraged and not dampened. Serious classrooms need not be somber ones; they can often be filled with rollicking laughter. Teachers need feel no inhibition in encouraging wit and humor; they both serve as a holiday from the often necessary gravity of learning and as one of the many paths to a fuller understanding of life.

Pleasure leads teachers to reveal their own joys and pleasures in learning and teaching. This means, of course, that teachers must have command of the knowledge they are trying to convey to their students. Yet it also means that in trying to instill in their students an enduring love of learning, teachers must impart their own love of it to those they are trying to teach. Only masochists are drawn to learning that tastes like soap. Most people need to have the satisfactions of knowledge exemplified for them; most learn best when the exactions of learning are shown to lead not just to knowledge but to knowledge that satisfies the human thirst for understanding. Teachers should not be self-conscious about revealing how knowledge has enriched their own lives and how their teaching is an expression of their desire to enrich others' lives too. On the contrary: they should try to exemplify the deep pleasure that their own continuing learning brings to them.

Pleasure means acknowledging the difficulties as well as the joys of learning. Just as happiness is deepened by the experience of sadness, so pleasure is always all the keener in proportion to the demands of its opposite—painful effort. To gain the satisfactions of learning, students must be confirmed in their struggles, frustrations, and disappointments in learning—and led to see the rich gains that come from the risks and costs of their hard work in seeking knowledge. When the difficulties of this work are granted and confirmed, students can accept their difficulties and so more readily keep up the struggle to learn. They are also prepared for the joys that spring from overcoming these difficulties.

Pleasure comes from witnessing the successes of former students as the years go by. Because all teaching is the preparation of students for their futures, some of the pleasure of teaching must be prospective: the anticipation of learning how one's former students have turned out. All teachers harbor the parental hope that they have contributed to their students' wisdom, happiness, and welfare. Teachers' greatest joys therefore originate in discovering that their students have done well, that their lives have been enriched by knowledge and understanding, and that they have been able to embrace life in all its fullness.

In its ultimate form, teachers' pleasure arises from the knowledge that their students have learned something from them. Surely it is understandable, even forgivably egotistical, for teachers to hope that their students understand what their teachers have given to them and for students to recall their teachers with affection and respect. What teacher will not envy Louis Germain, the teacher of the young Albert Camus, to whom the latter dedicated his Nobel Prize acceptance speech in 1957? In a letter attached to Camus's posthumously published autobiographical novel *The Last Man*, Camus addressed Germain, who had identified the youth's genius and, plucking him from the circumstances of his working-class family in Algiers, had introduced him to the world of knowledge: "When I learned the news of my award, my first thought, after my mother, was for you," Camus wrote Germain. "Without you, without the loving hand you extended to the poor little child that I was, without your teaching and your example, nothing of this would have happened. I do not make much of this sort of honor. But it at least presents an occasion to tell you what you have been and always are to me, and to assure you that your efforts, your work, and the generous heart that you offered me are always alive within one of your little schoolboys who, despite his age, has not ceased being your grateful student. I embrace you with all my strength."

There being probably no greater satisfaction for a teacher than this kind of encomium, it is the kind of rare pleasure that should be savored.

Pleasure is the one element of teaching whose acknowledgment can be made to seem illegitimate by our otherwise justified emphasis on the seriousness of learning. Yet without denying teachers' heavy responsibilities for the welfare of others and thus the gravity of their endeavor, we must also accept the place of enjoyment—both teachers' and students'—as an instrument of instruction as well as a goal of learning. A joyless classroom, a seminar of unrelieved sobriety, a cynical teacher of gloomy mien—all are impediments to learning, not stimuli. It is laughter, playfulness, and wit that by contrast open doors to the mind as well as the heart, that are indispensable ingredients of the art of teaching.

⇐⇐⇐

PROFESSOR KATHERINE SAUER was unusual. As a woman, she had struggled successfully to make her way in the traditionally masculine field of chemistry; as an American, she was considered odd because her only diversion was to read about the English game of cricket; and as a faculty member, she was found to be peculiar for agreeing time and time again to teach the basic course in chemistry to freshmen. Why, her colleagues asked, would she do that? "Because the students are so incompetent," she would answer. "Someone's got to stick the stuff down their throats." ("And how many of you," she would silently ask, "have the guts to do that?")

When a member of Professor Sauer's family remarked one day that the academy did not seem to elicit in its members a great generosity of spirit, she took that as a tribute. She could not imagine why she should think better of her students and colleagues than her professors had thought of her when she was fighting her way through graduate school, the first woman to do so in her field. They had put her to tests not required of the men in her program. Fearing that the results of her experiments were too good to be true for a woman, they had made her run them twice, sometimes three times; even her doctoral adviser, with whom she had collaborated in work that eventually gained him a Nobel Prize, remarked when she left to take her first position that she had accomplished much "for a woman."

Her first-term course was legendary on campus among those who had been there a while. Not knowing what was in store, her freshmen students, anticipating only hard work in a "hard" science course, were stunned that the material was easier than Professor Sauer. Most of them could learn the material well enough, but they could not please her. Without doubt, she knew her subject; her lecture-demonstrations were clear; the experiments she performed were illustrative of her subject; and the results always turned out as they should. But even when the demonstrations yielded explosions, or sudden bursts of light, or gooey messes, she stood by unsmiling. They thought the surprises fun; an old hand at the demonstrations, she found them boring and routine.

In the lab—most senior professors would not deign to conduct lab sessions, leaving them instead to graduate students— Katherine Sauer was unremitting in her solemnity. "If the students don't take this seriously," she thought, "how will they learn?" Amid loud pops, test tube contents turning bright colors, centrifuges separating sticky substances into distinct components, students were always in a state of expectancy and excitement. To their "How did that happen?" her response was always "What did you expect? That's what's supposed to happen." Her colleagues in English and history loved her. After a couple of terms of her unyielding sternness, most of her students decided to major in subjects in the humanities. She thought that a good thing: "No need for anyone but the most dedicated to pursue chemistry," she believed.

To the great confusion of her students, Dr. Sauer used many expressions associated, as they learned, with the game of cricket. She would hail a series of successful experiments as a "hat trick" or a "maiden over." She advised students to "keep a straight bat" when writing up their results. She called the difficulties they faced "sticky wickets." And she told those who took untenable positions that they were fielding "at silly mid on." Perhaps, her students thought, she was trying to make a joke. But the unrelieved seriousness of her demeanor eventually convinced them that these inscrutable comments, whatever their meaning, were consistent with her customary gravity.

Professor Sauer felt most at home with graduate students, especially those who were unmarried and could devote their entire lives to chemistry. This kind of devotion, in fact, she thought necessary of all graduate students, and she had gone so far in writing the university's guide to graduate studies as to recommend that married students live apart from their spouses. "Eros does not promote learning," she wrote. If few took her advice, many had to study with her. By that, she really meant "with her": she discouraged them from going off on their own until they had performed, reperformed, and performed yet again each experiment in her courses in physical chemistry. She had no use for the ways of one of her colleagues, beloved of all students. This man would enter his graduate history class the first day, tell his students that they could learn five times as much by reading in the library than listening to him for sixty minutes—and he meant it—then, with a twinkle in his eye and a little dog-eared notebook in his hand, enthrall his auditors with the history of the Portuguese caravel, of which, of course, no one in the world knew more. When his great work on Spanish exploration won the Pulitzer Prize, Professor Sauer attributed the award to the number of his colleagues on the prize panel, not the quality of his work.

Graduate students found that since there really was no way to please Professor Sauer, they would simply do the work and get out of physical chemistry as soon as they could. In her long years on the faculty, only two students had pursued their work with her. One had gone into his father's chemical company, the other into advising banks about underwriting loans for industrial research. She had trained no research chemists. Many of those who had passed through her courses had, however, achieved distinction in related specialties. One in particular had become truly notable and, after years of pathbreaking work, had, like Professor Sauer's own mentor, received a Nobel Prize. When this woman invited all her former teachers to celebrate with her, Professor Sauer did not attend the gathering. "She probably got the prize just because she's a woman," she complained to a colleague.

When the time came for her retirement, Professor Sauer abandoned both her teaching and her highly regarded work and took off for Great Britain, where she could finally indulge her passion for cricket. She had been putting aside funds for her retirement, planning to leave one life for another, for she had never taken even a single summer off to relearn the game that she had taken up as a teenager on vacation with her parents. She believed that, like eros, fun and recreation threatened learning and research. So when her last term on the faculty had ended, she closed up her laboratory without regret and departed for London—not, however, before her colleagues bade her farewell at a dinner at which many told stories about the department, though not about Professor Sauer, and a few even managed to laugh at jokes about themselves. When her colleagues presented her with the most ridiculous and appropriate gift they could think of—a new book, *Cricket for Chemists*—she admitted nothing. "I really don't know anything about the game," she said in thanking them. "Perhaps I should learn."

☙ Afterword

THOSE WHO HAVE READ what we have written about the constituent elements of teaching may be wondering by now whether achieving these standards is not beyond the reach of all but the rarest paragon. How can different teachers in a school or college classroom under differing conditions of instruction embody the qualities of character, heart, and mind that we have considered? How can those who teach without being formally employed to do so—as parents, say, or as physicians or scout leaders—summon these qualities in the normal course of their lives? And how can these elements be brought into some balance and the tensions often existing between them be resolved? How, for instance, can a teacher be empathetic and engaged, as called for by compassion, while being dispassionate, as often called for by ethics? Perhaps no one who teaches can be and do more than a fraction of what we have described as constituting teaching, and perhaps we are unreasonable in thinking, even hoping, that they can.

In fact, after reading what we have to say, readers may wonder why anyone would want to become or remain a teacher when the claims and responsibilities of being one are so many, so immediate, so urgent, and so weighty. Those who teach do so because they have known teaching's magical attraction to the spirit, to say nothing of the ego, and have known as students the lengths to which some teachers will go to help others, like themselves, to learn. They know that to convey to others the knowledge of any subject and to do so effectively are two of life's greatest joys.

Yet, as we must acknowledge, it is much easier to talk or write about teaching than it is actually to teach. The aspects of teaching that we have examined in this book are ideals—ends always to be sought if only rarely gained, their pursuit one of life's most difficult tasks. Those who have never taught probably cannot fully imagine the demands on energy, patience, and will imposed by classroom work. It is exacting labor, often lacking clear and tangible results and requiring teachers to begin all over again what they have already tried to do; and it has been made ever more demanding today by the trying social conditions that all too frequently challenge teachers and their students. We have therefore tried to make this book not so much an exploration of fixed truths or axioms as part of an open-ended exchange, among all of us who teach, about what we exemplify, do, convey, try to achieve, and struggle with every day, whether we are aware of it or not. In effect, we have tried to offer a better understanding of what teachers work at all their lives.

Some readers may have sensed in what we have written a certain gravity and earnestness about our subject, grounded in the conviction that teaching is a special occupation with special requirements and responsibilities. In that, they are right, because we believe teaching to be among the most serious and accountable activities of life, whose pursuit confers more moral and intellectual obligations on teachers than rights. It is a kind of civic office, whose occupants stand in for the human community and are expected to discharge certain agreed-upon responsibilities with special care.

Teaching is also the gift of one person to another. It is a compassionate extension of self in acknowledgment of the needs and aspirations of someone else, usually but not always younger than we are and always, for a time at least, dependent on us for some kind of knowledge. In that gift of self consists teaching's greatest satisfaction—the giving not so much of knowledge, which each person must acquire, as of habits of mind and heart and powers of thought.

If some conclude that we have taken teaching too seriously, others may think us naïve in believing, even hoping, that teachers will try to adopt the principles we have offered here. Do we ask too much? We think not. Because all teachers have been students, we are confident that most readers will recognize in what we have written the echoes of their own experiences, that they will recollect what it was like when they began to be students who at first found schoolwork and classroom assignments neither easy nor natural, and that they will therefore acknowledge that our depictions of the elements of teaching are applicable to their own lives. Many, perhaps most, teachers have taken up teaching because of the rich pleasures and satisfactions of their own youthful schooling; yet probably too seldom do they ask themselves what it was about their most favored and beloved teachers—among them no doubt parents, friends, and colleagues as well as classroom instructors—that so enriched their lives. In writing this book, we have tried to recall our own best teachers and thus to understand their great and special gifts. What we have written is in part our heartfelt tribute to them.

Our subject—the elements of teaching—has had to do with attitude, behavior, aspiration, and substance more than with means; our concerns have been with approaches, stances, and assumptions rather than with methods. This is not because we think techniques and ways of teaching are unimportant—precisely and emphatically the opposite. Instead, we have considered the qualities of character, bearing, and knowledge essential to teaching because we believe that very little attention has been paid to them in the literature of education. While there is no "one way" to teach, taken together the qualities of which we have written make up what good, sometimes great, teaching is.

Neither, of course, do the qualities about which we have written exhaust the subject. In writing about what we believe to be the principal elements of teaching, we have not meant to detract from those other elements that we have not selected for emphasis. We have discussed or implied many of them—such as devotion, honesty, courage, optimism, integrity, and spirit— along the way and hope that we have not forgotten any.

The gulf between the ideals represented by the elements of teaching considered in this book and the everyday practices of teachers may seem wide. But we do not believe that it is as wide as sometimes appears. We say this out of confidence in teachers' aspirations and out of our own experiences in the classroom. To be sure, few who have taught will deny that teaching can be fiendishly difficult and draining; those who have not taught in any sustained and continuous fashion are unlikely to know its exactions, its requisitions on one's inner resources, any more than they are likely to know its joys and satisfactions; and those who taught only in the past will probably not often have experienced the challenges that face instructors in the schools today. Few other human activities require of their practitioners so much in application, awareness, and energy that must be maintained from day to day, week to week, month to month, and year to year. Just getting the job done moderately well each day requires all that many teachers can bring to the task. Readers may therefore conclude that we are unrealistic in hoping that anyone can meet the high expectations we have written about or that our ideals have led us to overlook the conditions of the contemporary classroom; few people, perhaps none, they may say, can possess and employ all the qualities that we have explored and tried to illustrate in these pages. They will protest, moreover, that identifying standards is always easier than attaining them.

And yet it would be a serious mistake to presume that these standards are beyond the reach of most teachers, even when the challenges they face are taken into account; to do so, we believe, would be to misjudge the everyday practice of teaching and the routine achievements of so many teachers. For every act of teaching employs and exemplifies, either well or badly, one or more of the principal components of instruction of which we have written; all teaching is made up of some of these elements in some combination. Even without recognizing them, anyone who seeks to convey knowledge of any kind to another person is putting them into practice. What teachers must not be, we are certain, and what most are not, is indifferent to any one of these elements, any more than they can be indifferent to the minds and characters of each student they teach. Thus to distinguish and discuss each one of these elements is a necessary precondition to mastering the art of teaching but surely not an invitation to despair of possessing any single one of them or of all of them together.

What makes the art of teaching so difficult and excellent teaching so challenging—what may make what we have written seem so unreasonable—is not that one or two of the elements of teaching are called upon at all times in the classroom but that ideally all of them must be employed not singly or in pairs but all at once. Although the constituent elements of teaching can be distinguished in order to understand them better and to articulate some principles for their use, they are separable only for the purposes of understanding them. They are neither separable nor separate in fact. They join within each individual teacher as a manifestation of the teacher's identity. Medical students must study human anatomy one organ at a time, so that as experienced doctors diagnosing a patient's ailment they can make simultaneous use of their entire knowledge of physiology to treat that patient effectively. Similarly with teachers: as students of the art of teaching, they must examine each of its aspects one by one, but when they are teaching they must summon every quality of character, mind, and spirit they possess in order to accomplish their mission.

This effort requires a repeated extension of self equaled by few other callings. Teachers must bring the whole self, not simply learning, compassion, or imagination, to their work. All of us who have taught know that everything we put into our instruction is drawn from our own engagement with the world. The wonders and satisfactions of teaching result from our ongoing ability to call up our knowledge of life from our own inner store of understanding for the good of those we are trying to teach. The elements of teaching are thus no more than many of the elements of humanity that we all possess, and teachers are simply those who seek to make manifest what they know of humanity through their teaching. To ask them to explore the particular constituents of teaching is but to ask them to consider the inner resources they possess as human beings. In some respects, therefore, our analysis of teaching has been nothing more than an attempt to clarify the components of this extraordinary gift of self which teachers make every working day.

Teaching is made no easier by the paradox that although it does not take place in isolation, it is nevertheless a solitary act. In this regard it differs from many other human activities and professions. Though usually at work in the company of their students, teachers work alone in repeatedly bringing to bear every resource of knowledge, energy, and invention they possess not for their own good but to intensify their students' engagement with life through increasing their understanding of it. Though in doing so teachers are almost always part of a community of teachers in a school or university, they usually work apart from one another, each facing different groups of students of different minds and interests who are addressing different subjects.

If this book holds any value, perhaps it can help reduce some of the inherent isolation of teachers. Perhaps through talk, practice, observation, reading, and thought about the elements of teaching of which we have written, experienced and aspiring teachers will begin together and communally to consider the qualities of mind and spirit that constitute their everyday efforts. As teachers, we are not and probably never will be schooled in these qualities, nor trained in their application. But we can increase our awareness of them by examining them with others who are engaged in the same endeavors.

For while teaching is characteristically lonely, self-denying, exhausting work for individual teachers, its aims, components, and responsibilities are collaborative and consistent. Each teacher shares with every other the goals of shaping the characters of their students and helping them acquire the ability to fill their own minds. Each teacher strives to embody with every other teacher the elements that compose their teaching, and they bear the mutual obligation to protect the welfare of all their students. Each teacher shares a stake with every student's other teachers—including those who have preceded and those who will follow them—in the outcome of each student's learning. It follows that no single teacher can justifiably emphasize a single skill or quality to the exclusion of others. All teachers are responsible for teaching certain things in common and for attempting to do so with the same effort.

It is in these ways, therefore, that teaching is profoundly collegial and communal as well as solitary. A paradox? Not really. The subject may be history or biology, but the goals are the same: to awaken and develop the skills of observation, argument, and analysis; to teach accurate writing and speaking and careful reading; and to instill special qualities of mind and character—all while teaching a particular subject. And so, although the act of teaching may be, in its actions and effects, solitary, it is part of a collaborative effort; it carries with it shared obligations toward each student; its mutual elements carry with them mutual responsibilities. Teachers may not recognize this, and may not discuss it often, but this mutuality of ends and obligations—the universality of the elements of teaching—connects all teachers in a worldwide community of work and thought.

That community, of course, includes students. Mutuality characterizes the interests and responsibilities of students and teachers as much as it does the relationship between teachers. The relationship between teachers and students is reciprocal in a way not often acknowledged, for the elements of teaching that we have discussed here are the very same qualities that teachers hope to create in their students. This is why teachers must exemplify in their words and behavior, as well as in their lessons, the traits of mind and character they wish to instill in others. When successful, they are able to draw from their students the stimulus and strength to maintain their own standards of teaching.

In this way, teaching is a sharing of experience; and in the act of sharing, teachers are themselves enriched and emboldened to persevere. Certainly their concern for their students makes them anticipate the future with more hope than despair, with an optimism that is enviable and that ought to be contagious. It is their optimism, after all, that nourishes their students as they rise to the challenge that great teaching offers them. So when we say that the relationship between teacher and student is a reciprocal one, we mean that teaching is like a game of tennis: you need at least two players, one on each side of the net, and both engaged, to keep the ball in play.

In this book we have tried to describe the teacher's side of this engagement, the human qualities in teachers that encourage this active reciprocity. How students conduct themselves in order to make the best use of their teachers' gifts is a nice question—one, perhaps, for another book entirely. Or it may simply be left to the imagination of those who have read this one with, we hope, both pleasure and gain.